candyblankies

unique crochet for babies & toddlers

candi jensen

candyblankies

unique crochet for babies & toddlers

candi jensen

sixth&spring books

Sixth&Spring Books
233 Spring St.
New York, NY 10013

Editorial Director
Trisha Malcolm

Art Director
Chi Ling Moy

Photography
Dan Howell

Stylist
Mary Helt

Copy Editor
Jean Guirguis

Graphic Designer
Brenden Hitt

Technical Editors
Carla Scott
Pat Harste

Yarn Editor
Veronica Manno

Manager, Book Division
Michelle Lo

Production Manager
David Joinnides

President and Publisher, Sixth&Spring Books
Art Joinnides

Chairmen
Jay H. Stein
John E. Lehmann

Library of Congress Cataloging-in-Publication Data
Jensen, Candi
    Candy blankies : cuddly crochet for babies + toddlers / Candi Jensen.
            p.cm.
        ISBN 1-931543-41-0
    1. Crocheting—Patterns. 2. Blankets. Title.
    TT825 .J43 2004
    746.43'40432—dc21

                                            2003057294

            Manufactured in China

i n t r o d u c t i o n

Every baby needs a blankie,
a tale of two Johnnys.

Creativity is a funny thing. Sometimes you find ideas and inspiration in the things around you such as a color, texture or even a little glimpse of something out of the corner of your eye. More often than not, you expect something will turn out fabulous and once you get started, it doesn't resemble at all what you envisioned.

For me the most constant source of inspiration has been the babies and children in my neighborhood and most recently my new grandson, John Berg Vantress III, whom we call Johnny. He was certainly foremost in my thoughts when I sat down to work on the designs for this book, but the idea of blankies brought up another "Johnny" in my life, my son Jonathan.

Several years after I had my daughter Heather, I had this dream one night of adopting a son. When I awoke, being young and naive, that is just what I decided to do. We started the adoption process the next day. Having no idea how long this would take I picked up my crochet hook and started to make sweaters and blankets just like I had done when I was pregnant with my daughter. Well the process dragged on and 10½ months later we finally got the chance to meet our son, a 10½ month old named Jonathan (yes, I am convinced he was born on the night of my dream). When we walked into the room to pick him up little, Jonathan had only the clothes on his back and a ball in one hand and a blankie in the other; it was love at first sight. Little did I know then how much that blankie would mean to him. Even though I had made him several blankets and wanted desperately for him to choose one of those, he wouldn't part with his "blue blankie." In fact he had that blankie so long we were convinced he was going to go off to college with it in his pocket because by then it would have been so worn out only a few inches would have remained.

Jonathan did finally give up that blankie, although I won't tell you how old he was, and is now 33 and 6'5." We all joke and tease him about his attachment to that blanket now and he laughs right along with us, but he and I both know what that blanket really meant to him and how important it was to have something that he could depend on. Although he certainly doesn't need his blankie any more, I do notice that he looks

longingly at afghans once in awhile (could be a book in there somewhere).

When I started this book that vision of Jonathan with his blankie popped into my head, and I realized I wanted to come up with blanket designs that would someday become as cherished as "blue blankie" had been. My hope is that you will find inspiration in one or several of the blankies in this book and make them for your new little additions. Now that I have my new Johnny to design for, I'm sure one of the many blankies I have made for him will be dragged around and snuggled with for many years to come and just may become his "blue blankie."

jonathan and heather

it's a boy!
10/70

nursery magic
12/72

block party
14/74

it's a girl
16/76

cowboy blues
18/78

farm fresh
30/96

soothing note
32/98

tickled pink
34/100

english beat
36/102

special delivery
38/106

pretty in pink
50/120

true blue
52/122

rainbow bright
54/124

crème de la crème
56/126

pompom pleaser
58/128

c o n t e n t s

it's a boy!

Uncomplicated stitches, a vibrant palette and easy textures come together in this delightful confection of an afghan. Stitch the squares separately, sew them together and add a border. Voilà! It's a picture-perfect moment.

nursery magic

That's a wrap—crochet goes contemporary with this extra-special blanket worked in easy-going shades. Inspired by the classic argyle design, the blanket boasts an assortment of various-sized squares and chain-stitch embroidered accents. A single-crochet border completes the look.

block *party*

L avish a new arrival with this simple and easy-to-make cover up. With only nine simple half-double crochet squares to stitch up and sew together, this portable project is built for speed. Complete the look by adding a rich magenta border.

i t ' s   a   g i r l

Whimsical blocks in a kaleidoscope
of cheerful colors add up to
nursery-friendly fun. Each block is
stitched separately and crocheted with two
strands of yarn held together. Once the
blocks are sewn together, finish the
blanket with a shell stitch crochet trim.

c o w b

oy blues

After a day of play, round up your little one with this fun crochet blanket. Achieve the look of denim with simple contrast stitching, combine it with a funky cow print, and your little wrangler can curl up in style.

j e a n   d r e a m

Variegated blocks in muted shades
team up to lend a warm touch to
this chic kiddie essential. Squares are
stitched separately, then joined together
and decorated with yellow stitching.
A half-double crochet border offers a
handsome finish.

cre

Mooo-ve over baby pastels and make a bold statement with this cow-print blanket! A little intarsia makes for a fun, hip throw that will keep baby warm all through the night.

denim

dazzler

No need to settle for plain old colors. After a long day of play, your wee one will fall into sweet slumber with this denim-inspired creation. It works up in a flash using the half-double crochet stitch. Jazzy yellow stitching and a dark border make bold accents.

b e a r n e c e s s

This soft and cuddly blanket will have your baby smiling around the clock. Finishing touches like adorable crocheted ears and an embroidered smile make this blanket an instant classic that any child will love, and its simple construction means you'll love it too!

p u r r - f e c t i o n

Whip up a friendly feline throw your child will love. With crocheted ears and adorable embroidered whiskers, your little one will be begging to curl up for a catnap with this feline-friendly throw.

farm fresh

Crocheted in one piece, this wooly wonder will keep your little lamb warm all night long. The sheep are crocheted separately and sewn on, adding depth and dimension to this eye-catching blanket.

s o o t h i n g   *n o t e*

Stitched in one piece, the design showcases a lovely argyle-inspired pattern in perky tones. The enchanting single-crochet design can be done in a flash and it's a great project for busy crocheters.

t i c k l e d   *p i n k*

A sumptuous oh-so-cuddley blanket makes the ultimate statement in luxury. Composed of squares and triangles, this quick-to-crochet number works up in no time, leaving you more time to curl up with your tot.

english   beat

Wrap your baby in tradition with this argyle throw. Crocheted in snuggly soft cotton, this blanket is made in individual strips, then sewn together and accentuated with a chain stitch and complimentary border.

ial delivery

No need to sacrifice style for comfort—
let the snazzy stripes and bold palette
do all the work in this super-easy throw.

ripp

le   effect

Get ready to make some waves with this jewel-toned treasure that's sure to please your little gem. A carefree chevron pattern worked in vibrant berry hues is accented with whimsical pompoms.

blue marine

Naptime never felt this good!
Crocheted separately and then
stitched together, cheerful blocks in ocean
hues come together in this cradle-friendly
throw. An ivory border and embroidered
accents throughout make for a striking
contrast.

square dance

Quick stripes and easy patchwork squares work together in perfect harmony in this comely design. Crochet the stripe and gingham blocks individually, join them together, and then finish the look with a clean single-crochet stitch border.

ewee pizzazz

All newborns deserve a handmade blanket stitched with love. A winsome combination of checkered blocks in ivory and plum hues, handsome plaid stitching and pretty scalloped edges lends plenty of vintage charm to this classic heirloom treasure.

p a t t e r n   p l a y

This delightful little afghan is sure to be a favorite for any child and an instant heirloom to pass along to future generations. Bold colors, punchy patchwork and easy stitching work together in a striking combination. A decorative border makes a quick finish to the entire design.

in pink

Your wee one will relish the sweetest embrace of this light, lofty and very snuggle-worthy blanket. Warm to the touch, it features textured columns of thick and thin cables and a decorative crochet border.

⑥

t r u e   b l u e

Add some texture to your little one's life with this fetching blanket. Treble-crochet diamonds bring the rich color to life. Baby will love its soft cozy feel, and you'll love its simple pattern stitch repeat!

6

r a i n b o w   b r i g

*C*lassic white offers a simple setting for the colorful stripes on this pint-sized pleaser. A clever combination of long V-stitch and single-crochet stitching create subtle textural interest. It will quickly become your child's favorite.

crème de la

A fabric trim makes for a quick and clean edged binding on this no-fuss half double crochet blanket. Though toile was used, feel free to experiment with your favorite fabric patterns—the results just may surprise you.

crème

p o m p o m p l e

Pretty pompoms add verve to a charming baby blanket. Worked in half-double crochet stitch, the blanket features easy embroidery and single-crochet edging. In fact, the blanket is so easy to re-create, just stitch it up over a weekend for a little instant gratification.

b a b y   l o v e

Baby will have no problem catching
some zzz's—Single-crochet stitching,
a fanciful satin border, and rickrack trim
come together in this cradle charmer;
embroidery lends a delicate touch.

p e t a l   p r e t t y

Who wouldn't love this winsome vintage-style throw? Deceptively easy to make, transform an ordinary design into a lovely work of art with bouquets of budding flowers accented with dainty bobbles and a pretty scalloped edge.

f i n e   l i n e s

The key to this fast-paced charmer: Speedy stripes in varying widths and no-fuss half-double crochet stitch. Awash in dreamy pastels, it's cuddly soft and so simple to create, it makes a wonderful heartfelt gift.

navajo throw

Easy as 1-2-3, this rich serape-style throw is a cinch to crochet. Inspired by the sunsets of the Southwest, it's worked in eye-popping colors and makes a striking addition to most any nursery.

i n s t r u c t i o n s

i t ' s   a   b o y !

FINISHED MEASUREMENTS
• 32" x 32"/81 x 81cm

MATERIALS
• 4 1¾oz/50g balls (each approx 192yd/175m) of Dale of Norway Baby Ull (wool) each in #1 white (A) and #10 light periwinkle (C) (2)
• 3 balls in #11 light teal (B)
• 2 balls each in #19 dark teal (D), #8 periwinkle (E) and #34 bright green (F)
• Size H/8 (5mm) crochet hook or size to obtain gauge
• Bobbins

GAUGES
• 13 sts and 10 rows to 4"/10cm over hdc with 2 strands of yarn held tog and using size H/8 (5mm) hook.
• One square to 10"/25.5cm with 2 strands of yarn held tog and using size H/8 (5mm) hook.
Take time to check gauges.

NOTES
1 Work with 2 strands of yarn held tog throughout.
2 See page 139 for working color changes.
3 When working checkerboard pat, wind A, B, C, D, E and F onto separate bobbins.

SOLID SQUARE
(make 5)
With 2 strands of A, ch 35. **Row 1** Hdc in 3rd ch from hook and in each ch across—33 sts. Ch 2, turn. **Row 2** Hdc in each st across. Ch 2, turn. Rep row 2 for pat st and work until a total of 24 rows have been completed. Fasten off. Make 1 more square using A, 2 using B and 1 using C.

CHECKERBOARD SQUARE
(make 4)
Using 2 strands of yarn held tog throughout, work as foll: with B, ch 35.
Checkerboard pattern
Row 1 Hdc in 3rd ch from hook and in next 10 ch, change to D and hdc in next 11 ch, change to E and hdc in last 11 ch—33 sts. Ch 2, turn.
Rows 2, 4 and 6 With E, hdc in first 11 sts, with D, hdc in next 11 sts, with B, hdc in last 11 sts. Ch 2, turn.
Rows 3, 5 and 7 With B, hdc in first 11 sts, change to D, hdc in next 11 sts, change to E, hdc in last 11 sts. Ch 2, turn.
Row 8 Rep row 2. Join A, ch 2, turn.
Rows 9, 11, 13 and 15 With A, hdc in first 11 sts, change to C, hdc in next 11 sts, change to F, hdc in last 11 sts. Ch 2, turn.
Rows 10, 12, 14 and 16 With F, hdc in first 11 sts, change to C, hdc in next 11 sts, change to A, hdc in last 11 sts. Ch 2, turn. After row 16 is completed, join F, ch 2, turn.
Rows 17, 19, 21 and 23 With F, hdc in

first 11 sts, change to E, hdc in next 11 sts, change to A, hdc in last 11 sts. Ch 2, turn.
Rows 18, 20, 22 and 24 With A, hdc in first 11 sts, change to E, hdc in next 11 sts, change to F, hdc in last 11 sts. Ch 2, turn. After row 24 is completed, do not ch, fasten off.

FINISHING
Lightly block squares to measurements. Referring to photo, sew squares tog so center bottom and center top checkerboard squares are on their sides as shown.
Edging
From RS, join 2 strands of C with a sl st in center of any side edge. **Rnd 1** Ch 1, making sure that work lies flat, sc evenly around entire edge, working 3 sc in each corner. Join rnd with a sl st in first sc. **Rnd 2** Ch 4 (counts as 1 sc and ch 3), sk next 2 sts, sc in next st, *ch 3, sk next 2 sts, sc in next st; rep from * around working (sc, ch 3, sc) in each corner st. Join rnd with a sl st in first ch of ch-1. Fasten off. From RS, join 2 strands of E with a sl st in any corner ch-3 sp. **Rnd 3** Ch 3, work sc and 3 dc in next sp, *ch 3, work sc and 3 dc in next sp; rep from * around. Join rnd with a sl st in first ch of ch-3. Fasten off.

FINISHED MEASUREMENTS
• 34" x 34"/86.5 x 86.5cm

MATERIALS
• 4 4oz/125g hanks (each approx 256yd/235m) of Classic Elite Yarns Provence (cotton) in #2674 fiddlehead (MC) ▣
• 2 hanks in #2632 mad magenta (B)
• 1 hank each in #2648 blue slate (A) and #2603 morning mist (C)
• Size H/8 (5mm) crochet hook or size to obtain gauge
• Bobbins
• Yarn needle

GAUGES
• 14 sts and 12 rows to 4"/10cm over hdc using size H/8 (5mm) hook.
• One square to 10"/25.5cm using size H/8 (5mm) hook.
Take time to check gauges.

NOTES
1 See page 139 for working color changes.
2 When working colorblock squares, wind MC onto 2 bobbins and A and B onto separate bobbins.

3 See page 141 for embroidering chain-stitch.

SOLID SQUARE
(make 4)
With MC, ch 38. **Row 1** Hdc in 3rd ch from hook and in each ch across—36 sts. Ch 2, turn. **Row 2** Hdc in each st across. Ch 2, turn. Rep row 2 until total of 30 rows have been completed. Fasten off.

COLORBLOCK SQUARE
(make 5)
With MC, ch 38, change to A. **Row 1** Hdc in 3rd ch from hook and in next 3 ch, with MC, hdc in next 28 ch, with A, hdc in last 4 ch—36 sts. Ch 2, turn.
Rows 2 and 3 With A, hdc in first 4 sts, with MC, hdc in next 28 sts, with A, hdc in last 4 sts. Ch 2, turn. After row 3 has been completed, join MC, ch 2, turn.
Rows 4-10 With MC, hdc in each st across. Ch 2, turn.
Rows 11-16 With MC, hdc in first 14 sts, with B, hdc in next 8 sts, with MC, hdc in last 14 sts. Ch 2, turn.
Rows 17-23 Rep rows 4-10. After row 23

is completed, join A, ch 2, turn.

Rows 24-26 Rep row 2. After row 26 is completed, do not ch, fasten off.

FINISHING

Lightly block squares to measurements. Referring to photo, sew squares tog.

Embroidery

Take care to maintain st and row gauge when working chain-stitches. Referring to photo, use C to embroider diagonal lines of chain-stitches as shown.

Border

From RS, join B with a sl st in any corner.

Rnd 1 Ch 1, making sure that work lies flat, sc evenly around, working 3 sc in each corner. Join rnd with a sl st in first sc.

Rnds 2-5 Ch 1, sc in each around, working 3 sc in each corner st. Join rnd with a sl st in first sc. Fasten off.

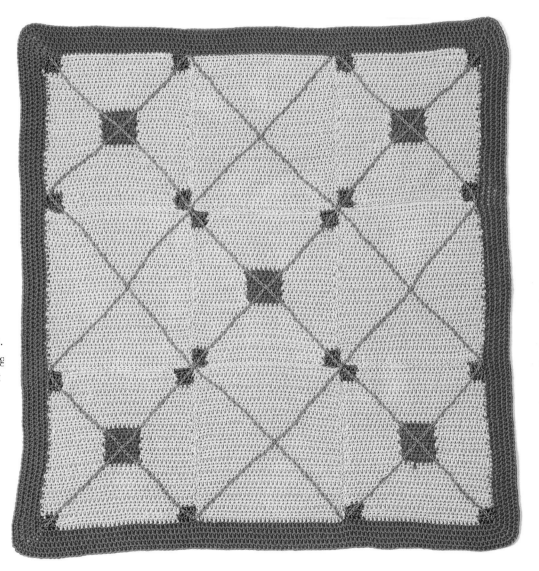

b l o c k   p a r t y

FINISHED MEASUREMENTS
- 31½" x 31½"/80 x 80cm

MATERIALS
- *2 1¾oz/50g (each approx 130yd/119m) of Jaeger HandKnits Matchmaker DK (wool) in #883 petal (A), #882 haze (B) and #881 trellis (C)*
- *1 ball in #876 clarice (D)*
- *Size G/6 (4.5mm) crochet hook or size to obtain gauge*

GAUGES
- 16 sts and 12 rows to 4"/10cm over hdc using size G/6 (4.5mm) hook.
- One square to 10"/25.5cm using size G/6 (4.5mm) hook.
- *Take time to check gauges.*

SQUARE

(make 9)

With A, ch 42. **Row 1** Hdc in 3rd ch from hook and in each ch across—40 sts. Ch 2, turn. **Row 2** Hdc in each st across. Ch 2, turn. Rep row 2 for pat st and work until piece measures 10"/25.5cm from beg. Fasten off. Make 2 more using A, and 3 each using B and C.

FINISHING

Lightly block squares to measurements. Referring to photo, sew squares tog.

Edging

From RS, join D with a sl st in center of any side edge. **Rnd 1** Ch 1, making sure that work lies flat, sc evenly around, working 3 sc in each corner. Join rnd with a sl st in first sc. **Rnd 2** Ch 3 (counts as 1 dc), work 2 dc in same st as joining, *sc in next st, dc in next 3 sts; rep from * around. Join rnd with a sl st in 3rd ch of ch-3. Fasten off.

i t ' s   a   g i r l

FINISHED MEASUREMENTS

• 34½" x 41"/87.5 x 104cm

MATERIALS

• 3 1¾oz/50g balls (each approx 192yd/175m) of Dale of Norway Baby Ull (wool) in #5 pink (A) ②
• 2 balls each in #1 white (B), #34 bright green (C), #11 light teal (D), #19 dark teal (E), #10 light periwinkle (F) and #8 periwinkle (G)
• Size H/8 (5mm) crochet hook or size to obtain gauge

GAUGES

• 13 sts and 10 rows to 4"/10cm over hdc with 2 strands of yarn held tog and using size H/8 (5mm) hook.
• One square to 6½"/16.5cm with 2 strands of yarn held tog and using size H/8 (5mm) hook.
Take time to check gauges.

NOTE

Work with 2 strands of yarn held tog throughout.

SQUARES

(make 30)
With 2 strands of A held tog, ch 24. **Row 1** Hdc in 3rd ch from hook and in each ch across—22 sts. Ch 2, turn. **Row 2** Hdc in each st across. Ch 2, turn. Rep row 2 for pat st and work until piece measures 6½"/16.5cm from beg. Fasten off. Make 5 more squares using A, 5 using B, 4 each using C, D, E and F, and 3 using G.

FINISHING

Lightly block squares to measurements. Referring to photo, sew squares tog alternating directions of squares, as shown.
Edging
From RS, join 2 strands of E with a sl st in center of any side edge. **Rnd 1** Ch 1, making sure that work lies flat, sc evenly around entire edge, working 3 sc in each

corner. Join rnd with a sl st in first sc. Fasten off. From RS, join 2 strands of A with a sl st in center st of any side edge. **Rnd 2** Ch 3 (counts as 1 hdc and ch 1), sk next st, sc in next st, *ch 1, sk next st, hdc in next st; rep from * around, working (hdc, ch 1, hdc, ch 1, hdc) in center sc of each corner. Join rnd with a sl st in 2nd ch of ch-3. **Rnd 3** Sl st in first ch-1 sp, ch 2 (counts as 1 hdc), work (ch 1, dc, ch 1, hdc) in same sp, *ch 1, work (hdc, ch 1, dc, ch 1, hdc) in next ch-1 sp; rep from * around, end ch 1. Join rnd with a sl st in 2nd ch of ch-2. Fasten off.

FINISHED MEASUREMENTS

• 30" x 34¾"/76 x 88cm (not including border)

MATERIALS

• 2 6oz/170g skeins (each approx 290yd/265m) of Red Heart®/Coats&Clark™ TLC Amoré (acrylic/nylon) in #3823 lake blue (A)
• 1 skein each in #3001 white (B) and #3002 black (C)
• 1 ball (each approx 350yd/320m) of Aunt Lydia Classic Crochet Cotton (cotton) in #421 goldenrod (D)
• Size H/8 (5mm) crochet hook or size to obtain gauge
• Bobbins
• Yarn needle

GAUGES

• 12 sts and 14 rows to 4"/10cm over sc and chart pat using size H/8 (5mm) hook.
• One block to 10" x 11½"/25.5 x 29cm using size H/8 (5mm) hook.
Take time to check gauges.

NOTES

1 Blanket can be made in one piece (version 1), as shown, or in separate blocks (version 2).
2 See page 139 for working color changes.
3 Wind B and C onto three separate bobbins each.
4 If making blanket in one piece, use a separate skein of A when working each A block.

VERSION 1

ONE PIECE

With A, ch 91. **Row 1 (RS)** Sc in 2nd ch from hook and in next 29 ch, change to B and beg chart at st 1 on row 1 and work in sc across next 30 ch, change to A and sc in last 30 ch—90 sts. Ch 1, turn. **Row 2** With A, sc in first 30 sts, change to B and work row 2 of chart, change to A and sc in last 30 sts. Ch 1, turn. Cont to work as established until row 40 of chart has been completed. Change to B, ch 1, turn. **Row 41** With B, beg chart at st 1 on row 1 and work in sc across next 30 sts, change to A and sc in next 30 sts, with B, beg chart at st 1 on row 1 and work in sc across last 30 sts. Ch 1, turn. Cont to work as established until row 40 of chart has been completed. Change to A, ch 1, turn. **Row 81** With A, sc in first 30 sts, change to B, beg chart at st 1 on row 1 and sc across next 30 sts, change to A and sc in last 30 sts. Ch 1, turn. Cont to work as established until row 40 of chart has been completed. Ch 1, turn. **Row 121** With A, sc in each st across. Fasten off.

VERSION 2

SOLID BLOCKS

(make 5)

With A, ch 31. **Row 1 (RS)** Sc in 2nd ch from hook and in each ch across—30 sts. Ch 1, turn. **Row 2** Sc in each st across. Ch 1, turn. Rep row 2 for pat st and work until a total of 40 rows have been completed. Fasten off.

COW PRINT BLOCKS

(make 4)

With B, ch 7, change to C and ch 16, change to B and ch 8. **Row 1 (RS)** With B, sc in 2nd ch from hook and in next 6 ch, with C, sc in next 16 ch, with B, sc in last 7 ch—30 sts. Ch 1, turn.

Beg chart

Row 2 (WS) Working in sc (with a ch 1 to turn), beg at st 30 and work to st 1. Cont to work as established to row 40. Fasten off.

FINISHING

Lightly block piece or blocks to measurements.

Pocket embroidery

Use four strands of D in needle throughout and make sure to maintain st and row gauge when stitching. Referring to chart and photo, embroider each A block using running stitches. Referring to photo, sew blocks tog for version 2.

Border

From RS, join A with a sl st in any corner. **Rnd 1** Ch 1, making sure that work lies flat, sc evenly around entire edge, working 3 sc in each corner. Join rnd with a sl st in first sc. **Rnds 2-6** Ch 1, sc in each around, working 3 sc in each corner st. Join rnd with a sl st in first sc. **Rnd 7** Ch 1, working from left to right, sc in each st around, working 2 sc in each corner st. Join rnd with a sl st in first sc. Fasten off.

Border embroidery

Use four strands of D in needle throughout and make sure to maintain st and row gauge when weaving. Working around rnd 1 of border, weave D under and over each st around, as shown. Rep weaving around rnd 3.

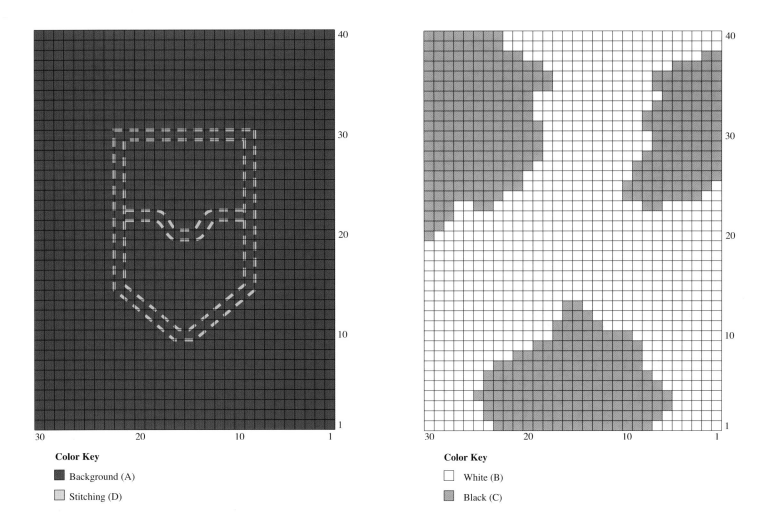

Color Key

■ Background (A)

□ Stitching (D)

Color Key

□ White (B)

■ Black (C)

j e a n   d r e a m

FINISHED MEASUREMENTS
• 37" x 37"/94 x 94cm

MATERIALS
• 2 3½ oz/100g balls (each approx 196yd/180m) of Bernat® Spinrite, Inc. Denim Style (acrylic/cotton) each in #3117 stonewash (A), #3044 sweatshirt (B) and #31081 indigo (C) (4)
• 1 ball (each approx 350yd/320m) of Aunt Lydia Classic Crochet Cotton (cotton) in #421 goldenrod (D) (1)
• Size I/9 (5.5mm) crochet hook or size to obtain gauge
• Yarn needle

GAUGES
• 10 sts and 7 rows to 4"/10cm over hdc using size I/9 (5.5mm) hook.
• One square to 11"/28cm using size I/9 (5.5mm) hook.
Take time to check gauges.

NOTE
See page 139 for working color changes.

SQUARE
(make 9)
With A, ch 30. **Row 1** Hdc in 3rd ch from hook and in each ch across 28 sts. Ch 2, turn. **Row 2** Hdc in each st across. Ch 2, turn. Rep row 2 for pat st and work until a total of 19 rows have been completed. Fasten off. Make 2 more using A and 3 each using B and C.

FINISHING
Lightly block pieces to measurements. Referring to photo, sew squares tog.
Border
From RS, join A with a sl st in center of any side edge. **Rnd 1** Ch 2, making sure that work lies flat, hdc evenly around entire edge, working 3 hdc in each corner. Join rnd with a sl st in first hdc. **Rnd 2** Ch 2, hdc in each st around, working (2 hdc, ch 1, 2 hdc) in center hdc of each corner. Join rnd with a sl st in first hdc changing to B. **Rnds 3 and 4** Ch 2, hdc in each st around, working (2 hdc, ch 1, 2 hdc) in ch-1 sp of each corner. Join rnd with a sl st in first hdc. After rnd 4 is completed, join rnd with a sl st in first hdc changing to C. **Rnd 5 and 6** Rep rnd 3 and 4. After rnd 6 is completed, join rnd with a sl st in first hdc, fasten off.
Embroidery
Refer to photo. Use three strands of D in needle throughout and make sure to maintain st and row gauge when weaving. Working around rnd 1 of border, weave B under and over every 2 sts around. For vertical stitching lines, weave under and over each row between last 2 sts of RH and center squares, then between first 2 sts of center and LH squares. For horizontal stitching lines, weave under and over every 2 sts along row 18 of bottom and center row of squares, then along row 2 of center and top row of squares.

FINISHED MEASUREMENTS

• 32" x 34¾"/81 x 88cm (not including border)

MATERIALS

• 2 6oz/170g skeins (each approx 290yd/ 265m) of Red Heart®/ Coats&Clark™ TLC Amoré (acrylic/nylon) in #3001 white (A)
• 1 skein each in #3002 black (B) and #3823 lake blue (C) ③
• 1 ball (each approx 350yd/320m) of Aunt Lydia Classic Crochet Cotton (cotton) in #421 goldenrod (D) ①
• Size H/8 (5mm) crochet hook or size to obtain gauge
• Bobbins
• Yarn needle

GAUGE

12 sts and 14 rows to 4"/10cm over sc and chart pat using size H/8 (5mm) hook.
Take time to check gauge.

NOTES

1 See page 139 for working color changes.
2 Wind A and B onto three separate bobbins each.

BLANKET

With A, ch 97. **Foundation row (WS)** Sc in 2nd ch from hook and in each ch across— 96 sts. Ch 1, turn.

Beg chart

Row 1 (RS) Working in sc (with a ch 1 to turn), beg at st 1 and work to st 96. Cont to work as established to row 120. Join A, ch 1, turn. Work even for 1 row. Fasten off.

FINISHING

Lightly block piece to measurements.

Border

From RS, join C with a sl st in any corner.

Rnd 1 Ch 1, making sure that work lies flat, sc evenly around entire edge, working 3 sc in each corner. Join rnd with a sl st in first sc. **Rnds 2-6** Ch 1, sc in each around, working 3 sc in each corner st. Join rnd with a sl st in first sc. After rnd 6 is completed, join rnd with a sl st in first sc, fasten off.

Embroidery

Use four strands of D in needle throughout and make sure to maintain st and row gauge when weaving. Working around rnd 3 of border, weave D under and over each st around, as shown. Rep weaving around rnd 5.

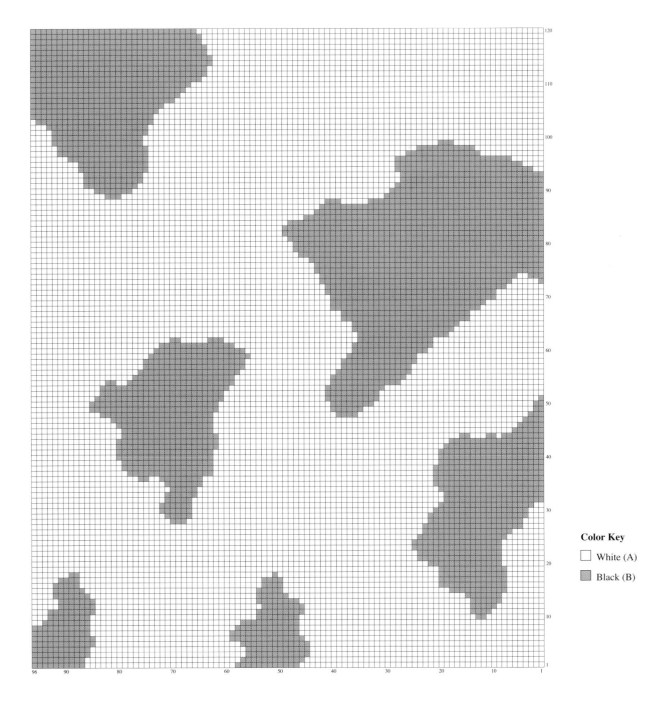

Color Key

☐ White (A)

▨ Black (B)

d e n i m   d a z z l e r

FINISHED MEASUREMENTS
• 32" x 36"/81 x 91.5cm (not including border)

MATERIALS
• 3 3½oz/100g balls (each approx 196yd/180m) of Bernat® Spinrite, Inc. Denim Style (acrylic/cotton) in #3044 sweatshirt (MC) (4)
• 1 ball in #3108 indigo (A)
• 1 ball (each approx 350yd/320m) of Aunt Lydia Classic Crochet Cotton (cotton) in #421 goldenrod (B) (1)
• Size I/9 (5.5mm) crochet hook or size to obtain gauge
• Yarn needle

GAUGE
10 sts and 7 rows to 4"/10cm over hdc using size I/9 (5.5mm) hook.
Take time to check gauge.

BLANKET
With MC, ch 82. **Row 1** Hdc in 3rd ch from hook and in each ch across—80 sts. Ch 2, turn. **Row 2** Hdc in each st across. Ch 2, turn. Rep row 2 until piece measures 36"/91.5cm from beg. Fasten off.

FINISHING
Lightly block piece to measurements.
Border
From RS, join A with a sl st in center of any side edge. **Rnd 1** Ch 1, making sure that work lies flat, sc evenly around entire edge, working 3 sc in each corner. Join rnd with a sl st in first sc. **Rnd 2** Ch 2, turn. Hdc in each st around, working (2 hdc, ch 1, 2 hdc) in center sc of each corner. Join rnd with a sl st in first hdc. **Rnd 3** Ch 1, turn. Sc in each st around, working 3 sc in each corner ch-1 sp. Join rnd with a sl st in first sc. Rep rnds 2 and 3 once more. Fasten off.
Embroidery
Use three strands of B in needle throughout and make sure to maintain st and row gauge when weaving. Working around rnd 1 of border, weave B under and over each st around, as shown. Rep weaving around rnd 3.

FINISHED MEASURMENTS
• 35" x 35"/89 x 89cm

MATERIALS
• 3 1¾ oz/50g balls (each approx 114yd/105m) of Wendy/Berroco, Inc. Velvet Touch (nylon) in #1215 blue (C) 4
• 2 balls each in #1200 white (A) and #2001 tan (B)
• Sportweight yarn in black for embroidery
• Size H/8 (5mm) crochet hook or size to obtain gauge
• Bobbins
• Yarn needle

GAUGES
• 12 sts and 10 rows to 4"/10cm over hdc using size H/8 (5mm) hook.
• One square to 9½"/24cm using size H/8 (5mm) hook.
Take time to check gauges.

NOTES
1 See page 139 for working color changes.
2 Wind A onto two separate bobbins and B onto one bobbin.

SQUARE
(make 9)
With A, ch 30. **Row 1 (WS)** Hdc in 3rd ch from hook and in each ch across—28 sts. Ch 2, turn. **Rows 2-5** Hdc in each st across. Ch 2, turn.

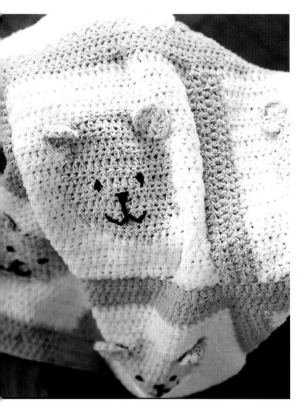

Beg chart

Row 6 (RS) Beg at st 1 and work to st 28. Work as established until row 24 is completed. Fasten off.

EARS

(make 18)

With B, ch 2. **Row 1** In 2nd ch from hook, work (sc, 2 hdc, dc, 2 hdc, sc). Ch 1, turn. **Row 2** Sc in first st, work 2 hdc in each of next 2 sts, dc in next st, work 2 hdc in each of next 2 sts, sc in last st. Fasten off leaving a long tail for sewing.

FINISHING

Lighty block squares to measurements.

Embroidery

Refer to photo. Using a single strand of black, embroider eyes and nose in satin stitch, center of lip in straight stitch and muzzle outlines in open lazy-daisy stitch. Sew on ears.

Left side border

Position a square so LH edge is at top. From RS, join C with a sl st in side edge of last row, ch 2. **Row 1** Work 1 hdc in each row to bottom edge—24 sts. Ch 2, turn. **Rows 2-5** Hdc in each st across. Ch 2, turn. After row 5 is completed, do not ch, fasten off. Work border on 5 more squares. Place 2 squares with borders side by side, then place a plain square on the left. Sew side edge of these squares tog forming a strip. Rep twice more.

Horizontal border

From RS, join C with a sl st in top RH edge of one strip. **Row 1** Work 1 hdc in each st across entire top edge—94 sts. Ch 2, turn.

Rows 2-5 Hdc in each st across. Ch 2, turn. After row 5 is completed, do not ch, fasten off. Rep once more. Place one strip with border above another strip with border, then place plain strip above them. Sew strips tog, as shown.

Outer border

From RS, join C with a sl st in center of any side edge. **Rnd 1** Ch 2, making sure that work lies flat, hdc evely around entire edge working 3 hdc in each corner. Join rnd with a sl st in first hdc. **Rnds 2-5** Ch 2, hdc in each st around, working 3 hdc in each corner st. Join rnd with a sl st in first hdc. After rnd 5 is completed, fasten off.

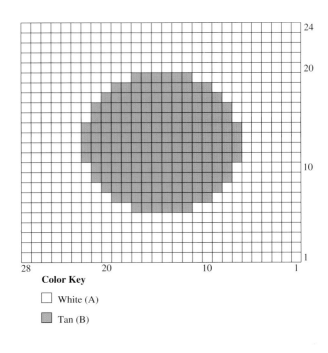

Color Key

☐ White (A)

▧ Tan (B)

p u r r - f e c t i o n

FINISHED MEASURMENTS
• 35" x 35"/89 x 89cm

MATERIALS
• 5 1¾oz/50g balls (each approx 114yd/105m) of Wendy/Berroco, Inc. Velvet Touch (nylon) in #1209 pink (MC) (4)
• 2 balls in #1200 white (CC)
• Sportweight yarn in medium blue, medium pink and tan for embroidery
• Size H/8 (5mm) crochet hook or size to obtain gauge
• Bobbins
• Yarn needle
• Pink sewing thread
• Sewing needle

GAUGES
• 12 sts and 10 rows to 4"/10cm over hdc using size H/8 (5mm) hook.
• One square 9½"/24cm using size H/8 (5mm) hook.
Take time to check gauges.

NOTES
1 See page 139 for working color changes.
2 Wind CC onto two separate bobbins and MC onto one bobbin.

SQUARE
(make 9)
With CC, ch 30. **Row 1 (WS)** Hdc in 3rd ch from hook and in each ch across—28 sts. Ch 2, turn. **Rows 2-5** Hdc in each st across. Ch 2, turn.

Beg chart

Row 6 (RS) Beg at st 1 and work to st 28. Work as established until row 24 is completed. Fasten off.

EARS

(make 18)

With MC, ch 2. **Row 1** In 2nd ch from hook, work (sc, 2 hdc, dc, 2 hdc, sc). Ch 1, turn. **Row 2** Sc in first st, work 2 hdc in next st, 2 dc in next st, tr in next st, 2 dc in next st, 2 hdc in next st, sc in last st. Fasten off leaving a long tail for sewing onto blanket.

FINISHING

Lighty block squares to measurements.

Embroidery

Refer to photo and use a single strand of yarn in needle. Working in satin stitch, embroider eyes using medium blue and nose using medium pink. Using medium pink, embroider center of lip in straight stitch and cheek outlines in open lazy-daisy stitch. Using tan, embroider whiskers in straight stitch.

Ears

Using pink thread and sewing needle, pinch top of ear tog to form a point; sew point to secure. Sew on ears as shown.

Left side border

Position a square so LH edge is at top. From RS, join MC with a sl in side edge of last row, ch 2. **Row 1** Work 1 hdc in each row to bottom edge—24 sts. Ch 2, turn. **Rows 2-5** Hdc in each st across. Ch 2, turn. After row 5 is completed, do not ch, fasten off. Work border on 5 more squares. Place 2 squares with borders side by side, then place a plain square on the left. Sew side edge of these squares tog forming a strip. Rep twice more.

Horizontal border

From RS, join MC with a sl st in top RH edge of one strip. **Row 1** Work 1 hdc in each st across entire top edge—94 sts. Ch 2, turn. **Rows 2-5** Hdc in each st across. Ch 2, turn. After row 5 is completed, do not ch, fasten off. Rep once more. Place one strip with border above another strip with border, then place plain strip above them. Sew strips tog, as shown.

Outer border

From RS, join MC with a sl st in center of any side edge. **Rnd 1** Ch 2, making sure that work lies flat, hdc evenly around entire edge working 3 hdc in each corner. Join rnd with a sl st in first hdc. **Rnds 2-5** Ch 2, hdc in each st around, working 3 hdc in each corner st. Join rnd with a sl st in first hdc. After rnd 5 is completed, fasten off.

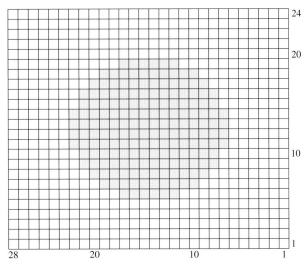

Color Key

☐ White (CC)

☐ Pink (MC)

f a r m   f r e s h

FINISHED MEASUREMENTS

• 36" x 38"/ 91.5 x 96.5cm (not including border)

MATERIALS

• 5 5oz/143g skeins (each approx 302yd/ 277m) of Red Heart®/ Coats&Clark™ Kids (acrylic) in #2652 lime (MC) ⬤4
• 1 6oz/170g skeins (each approx 148yd/135m) of Red Heart®/Coats&Clark™ Light and Lofty (acrylic) each in #9311 cloud (A) and #9312 onyx (B) ⬤4
• Worsted weight yarn in white and black for embroidery
• Size H/8 and K/10½ (5 and 7mm) crochet hooks or size to obtain gauge
• Yarn needle

GAUGES

• 12 sts and 10 rows to 4"/10cm over pat st using MC and size H/8 (5mm) hook.
• 10 sts and 8 rows to 4"/10cm over sc using A and size K/10½ (7mm) hook.
Take time to check gauges.

BLANKET

With H/8 (5mm) hook and MC, ch 109. **Row 1** Sc in 2nd ch from hook, dc in next ch, * sc in next ch, dc in next ch; rep from * across—108 sts. Ch 1, turn. **Row 2** *Sc in next st, dc in next st; rep from * across. Ch 1, turn. Rep row 2 for pat st and work until piece measures 38"/96.5cm from beg. Fasten off.

SHEEP

(make 8)

With K/10½ (7mm) hook and A, ch 9. **Row 1** Sc in 2nd ch from hook and in each ch across—8 sts. Ch 1, turn. **Row 2** Work 2 sc in first st, sc in next 6 sts, work 2 sc in last st—10 sts. Ch 1, turn. **Row 3** Work 2 sc in first st, sc in next 8 sts, work 2 sc in last st—12 sts. Ch 1, turn. **Row 4** Sc in first 8 sts, [dec 1 st over next 2 sts] twice—10 sts. Ch 1, turn. **Row 5** Dec 1 st over first 2 sts, sc in next st, hdc in next st, sc in next 2 sts, sl st in next st, sc in next 2 sts, do not work last st—8 sts. Ch 1, turn. **Row 6** Work 2 sc in first st, sc in next st—3 sts. Ch 1, turn. **Row 7** Sc in first 2 sts, work 3 sc in last st—5 sts. Ch 1, turn. **Row 8** Dec 1 st over first 2 sts, hdc in next st, dec 1 st over last 2 sts—3 sts. Fasten off. Make 6 more sheep using A and 1 using B.

FINISHING

Lightly block blanket to measurements. Referring to photo, sew on sheep.

Embroidery

For white sheep, use black worsted weight yarn. Make French knot eyes, and chain stitch ears and legs, as shown. For black sheep, use white worsted weight yarn and work as for white sheep.

Fence border

From RS with H/8 (5mm) hook, join MC with a sl st in first st or row after any corner. **Rnd 1** Ch 1, making sure that work lies flat, sc evenly around entire edge, working 3 sc in each corner. Join rnd with a sl st in first sc. **Rnd 2** Ch 3, *ch 1, sk next st, dc in next st; rep from * around, working (dc, ch 1, dc, ch 1, dc) in center sc of each corner. Join rnd with a sl st in 3rd ch of ch-3. **Rnd 3** Ch 3, *ch 1, sk next ch-1 sp, dc in next dc; rep from * around, working (dc, ch 1, dc, ch 1, dc) in center dc of each corner. Join rnd with a sl st in 3rd ch of ch-3. **Rnd 4** Ch 1, sc in same st as joining, sc in each dc and ch-1 sp around, working 3 sc in center dc of each corner. Join rnd with a sl st in first sc. Fasten off.

FINISHED MEASUREMENTS

• 31" x 34"/78.5 x 86.5cm (without border)

MATERIALS

• 3 4oz/125g hanks (each approx 256yd/234m) of Classic Elite Yarns Provence (cotton) in #2608 light blue (MC) 〔3〕
• 1 hank each in #2681 bright green (A), #2648 medium blue (B) and #2692 dark blue (C)
• Size H/8 (5mm) crochet hook or size to obtain gauge
• Bobbins
• Yarn needle

GAUGE

14 sts and 12 rows to 4"/10cm over hdc using size H/8 (5mm) hook.
Take time to check gauge.

NOTES

1 Blanket is made in one piece.
2 See page 139 for working color changes.
3 Wind MC and A onto three separate bobbins each and B onto two separate bobbins.
4 When working all MC rows, work from a hank of yarn rather than from a bobbin.

BLANKET

With MC, ch 110. **Row 1 (RS)** Hdc in 3rd ch from hook and in each ch across—108 sts. Ch 2, turn. **Row 2** Hdc in each st across. Join A, ch 2, turn.

Color Pattern

Rows 3-8 With A, hdc in first 8 sts, with MC, hdc in next 42 sts, with A, hdc in next 8 sts, with MC, hdc in next 42 sts, with A, hdc in last 8 sts. Ch 2 turn. After row 8 is completed, join MC, ch 2, turn.

Rows 9-22 With MC, hdc in each st across. Ch 2, turn.

Rows 23-34 With MC, hdc in first 18 sts, with B, hdc in next 14 sts, with MC, hdc in next 44 sts, with B, hdc in next 14 sts, with MC, hdc in last 18 st. Ch 2, turn.

Rows 35-48 With MC, hdc in each st across. Ch 2, turn. After row 48 is completed, join A, ch 2, turn.

Rows 49-54 Rep row 3. After row 54 is completed, join MC, ch 2, turn.

Rows 55-68 With MC, hdc in each st across. Ch 2, turn.

Rows 69-80 Rep row 23.

Rows 81-94 With MC, hdc in each st across. Ch 2, turn. After row 94 is completed, join A, ch 2, turn.

Rows 95-100 Rep row 3. After row 100 is completed, join MC, ch 2, turn.

Rows 101 and 102 With MC, hdc in each st across. Ch 2, turn. After row 102 is completed, do no ch, fasten off.

FINISHING

Lightly block piece to measurements.

Embroidery

Refer to photo. Use yarn doubled in needle throughout and make sure to maintain st and row gauge when weaving. Weave under and over every 2 sts or rows. For horizontal and vertical stitching lines, use B to weave across center of A blocks and use A to weave across center of B blocks, as shown.

Border

From RS, join C with a sl st in center of one side edge. **Rnd 1** Ch 1, making sure that work lies flat, sc evenly around entire edge, working 3 sc in each corner. Join rnd with a sl st in first sc. **Rnds 2-5** Ch 2, hdc in each st around, working 3 hdc in each corner. Join rnd with a sl st in first hdc. After rnd 5 is completed, join rnd with a sl st in first hdc, fasten off.

t i c k l e d   p i n k

FINISHED MEASUREMENTS

• 36" x 36"/91.5 x 91.5cm (not including border)

MATERIALS

• 5 1¾oz/50g balls (approx 137yd/125m) of Lion Brand Yarn Co. Polarspun (polyester) each in #101 pink (A) and #157 polar yellow (B)
• 1 ball in #100 snow white (C)
• Size H/8 (5mm) crochet hook or size to obtain gauge
• Yarn needle

GAUGE

One square to 12"/30.5cm using size H/8 (5mm) hook.
Take time to check gauge.

SQUARE

(make 5)

With A, ch 4 loosely. Join ch with a sl st forming a ring.

Rnd 1 (WS) Ch 2 (counts as 1 hdc), work 2 hdc in ring, [ch 2 for corner sp, 3 hdc in ring] 3 times, end ch 2 for last corner sp. Join rnd with a sl st in 2nd ch of ch-2. Turn. **Rnd 2 (RS)** Ch 3 (counts as 1 dc), [work (2 dc, ch 2, 2 dc) in corner ch-2 sp, dc in next 3 sts] 3 times, end work (2 dc, ch 2, 2 dc) in corner ch-2 sp, dc in last 2 sts—7 dc each side. Join rnd with a sl st in 3rd ch of ch-3. Turn.

Rnd 3 Ch 2 (counts as 1 hdc), hdc in next 5 sts, [work (2 hdc, ch 2, 2 hdc) in corner ch-2 sp, hdc in next 7 sts] 3 times, end work (2 hdc, ch 2, 2 hdc) in corner ch-2 sp, hdc in last st—11 hdc each side. Join rnd with a sl st in 2nd ch of ch-2. Turn.

Rnd 4 Ch 3 (counts as 1 dc), dc in next 2 sts, [work (2 dc, ch 2, 2 dc) in corner ch-2 sp, dc in next 11 sts] 3 times, end work (2 dc, ch 2, 2 dc) in corner ch-2 sp, dc in last 8 sts—15 dc each side. Join rnd with a sl st in 3rd ch of ch-3. Turn.

Rnd 5 Ch 2 (counts as 1 hdc), hdc in next 10 sts, [work (2 hdc, ch 2, 2 hdc) in corner ch-2 sp, hdc in next 15 sts] 3 times, end work (2 hdc, ch 2, 2 hdc) in corner ch-2 sp, hdc in last 4 sts—19 hdc each side. Join rnd with a sl st in 2nd ch of ch-2. Turn.

Rnd 6 Ch 3 (counts as 1 dc), dc in each st to corner, [work (2 dc, ch 2, 2 dc) in corner ch-2 sp, dc in each st to corner] 3 times, end work (2 dc, ch 2, 2 dc) in corner ch-2 sp, dc in each st to beg—23 dc each side. Join rnd with a sl st in 3rd ch of ch-3. Turn.

Rnd 7 Ch 2 (counts as 1 hdc), hdc in each st to corner, [work (2 hdc, ch 2, 2 hdc) in corner ch-2 sp, hdc in each st to corner] 3 times, end work (2 hdc, ch 2, 2 hdc) in corner ch-2 sp, hdc in each st to beg—27 hdc each side. Join rnd with a sl st in 2nd ch of ch-2. Turn. Cont to rep rows 6 and 7 (having 4 additional sts on each side every rnd) until square measures 12"/30.5cm. Fasten off. Make 3 more using A and make 1 using B.

SIDE HALF-SQUARE

(make 4)

With B, ch 4 loosely. Join ch with a sl st forming a ring.

Row 1 (WS) Ch 3 loosely (counts as 1 hdc and ch 1), work 2 hdc in ring, ch 2 for corner sp, work 2 hdc in ring, ch 1, hdc in ring for side sp. Turn.

Row 2 (RS) Ch 4 loosely (counts as 1 dc and ch 1), work 2 dc in ch-1 sp, dc in each st to corner sp, work (2 dc, ch 2, 2 dc) in corner ch-2 sp, dc in each st to ch-1 sp, work 2 dc in ch-1 sp, end ch 1, dc in 2nd ch of ch-3 of previous row——7 dc each side. Turn.

Row 3 Ch 3 loosely (counts as 1 hdc and ch 1), work 2 hdc in ch-1 sp, hdc in each st to ch-2 sp, work (2 hdc, ch 2, 2 hdc) in corner ch-2 sp, hdc in each t to ch-1 sp, work 2 hdc in ch-1 sp, end ch 1, hdc in 3rd ch of ch-4 of previous row——11 hdc each side. Turn. Cont to rep rows 2 and 3 (having 4 additional sts on each side every row) until sides of triangle measure 12"/30.5cm. Fasten off. Make 3 more using B.

CORNER HALF-SQUARE

(make 4)
Work as for side half-square until base of triangle measures 12"/30.5cm across.

FINISHING

Lightly block pieces to measurements. Referring to photo, whipstitch pieces tog as shown.

Blanket embroidery

Take care to maintain st and row gauge when working chain-stitches. Referring to photo, use C to embroider diagonal chain-stitch lines; as shown.

Border

From RS, join C with a sl st in center of any side edge. **Rnd 1** Ch 1, making sure

that work lies flat, sc evenly around entire edge, working 3 sc in each corner. Join rnd with a sl st in first sc. Turn. **Rnds 2-4** Ch 2, hdc in each st around, working 3 hdc in center st of each corner. Join rnd with a sl st on first hdc. Turn. When rnd 4 is completed, join rnd with a sl st on first hdc, fasten off.

Border embroidery

Take care to maintain st and row gauge when working chain-stitches. Referring to photo, use C to embroider a line of chain-stitchs along rnd 2; as shown.

e n g l i s h   b e a t

• 31" x 34½"/78.5 x 87.5cm (not including border)

MATERIALS

• 2 4oz/125g hanks (each approx 256yd/234m) of Classic Elite Yarns Provence (cotton) each in #2612 yellow (A) and #2647 medium blue (B) **3**
• 1 hank in #2608 light blue (C)
• Size H/8 (5mm) crochet hook or size to obtain gauge
• Bobbins
• Yarn needle

GAUGE

14 sts and 10 rows to 4"/10cm over hdc using size H/8 (5mm) hook.
Take time to check gauge.

NOTES

1 Blanket is made in three strips.
2 See page 139 for working color changes.
3 Wind A onto two separate bobbins.

STRIPS 1 AND 3

With A, ch 41. **Row 1 (RS)** Hdc in 3rd ch from hook and in each ch across—39 sts. Ch 2, turn. **Row 2** Hdc in each st across. Ch 2, turn. Rep row 2 for pat st.

Beg chart
Row 3 (RS) Beg at st 1 and work to st 39. Cont to work as established to row 78. Fasten off.

STRIP 2

Work as for strip 1 and 2, but working rows 3-39 using C instead of B and rows 40-76 using B instead of C.

FINISHING

Lightly block strips to measurements. Referring to photo, sew strips tog as shown.

Embroidery
Take care to maintain st and row gauge when working chain-stitches. Referring to photo, use C to embroider diagonal lines of chain-stitches across B diamonds and B to embroider diagonal lines of chain-stitches across C diamonds, as shown.

Border

From RS, join A with a sl st in center of any side edge. **Rnd 1** Ch 2, making sure that work lies flat, hdc evenly around entire edge, working 3 hdc in each corner. Join rnd with a sl st in first hdc. Fasten off. From RS, join B with a sl st in center st of any side edge. **Rnd 2** Ch 1, sc in same st as joining, *ch 1, sk next st, sc in next st; rep from * around, working (sc, ch 3, sc) in each corner st. Join rnd with a sl st in ch-1. Sl st in next ch-1 sp, turn. **Rnd 3 (WS)** Ch 2, hdc in same st as sl st, work 2 hdc in each ch-1 sp around, working (2 hdc, ch 2, 2 hdc) in each corner ch-3 sp. Join rnd with a sl st in 2nd ch of ch-2. Ch 1, turn. **Rnd 4** Working through back lps, sc in next st, *ch 1, sk next st, sc in next st; rep from * around, working (sc, ch 3, sc) in each corner ch-2 sp. Join rnd with a sl st in first sc. Sl st to next ch-1 sp, turn. **Rnd 5 (WS)** Rep rnd 3. Join rnd with a sl st in 2nd ch of ch-2. **Rnd 6 (WS)** Ch 1, working through front lps, sc in each st around, working (2 sc, ch 2, 2 sc) in each corner ch-2 sp. Join rnd with a sl st in first sc. Fasten off.

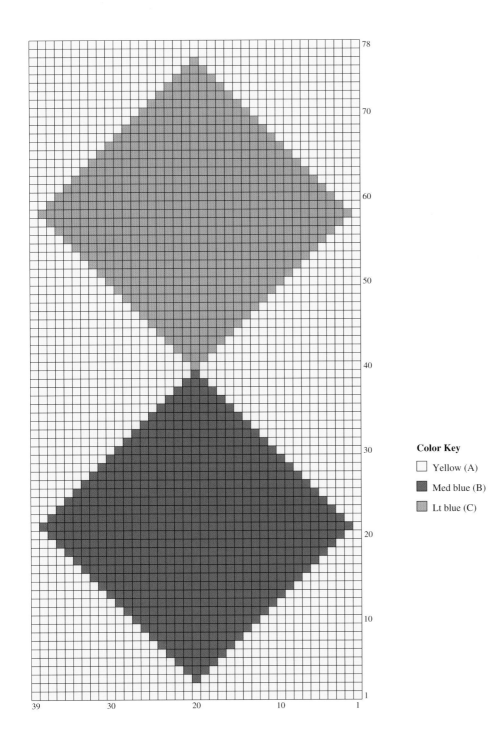

Color Key

☐ Yellow (A)

■ Med blue (B)

■ Lt blue (C)

FINISHED MEASUREMENTS

• 34" x 34"/86.5 x 86.5cm (not including edging)

MATERIALS

• 4 3oz/86g skeins (each approx 175yd/160m) of Caron International Simply Soft (acrylic) in #2614 soft pink (MC) **3**
• 2 skeins in #9701 white (B)
• 1 skein each in #9740 soft grey (A) and #9729 red (C)
• Size H/8 (5mm) crochet hook or size to obtain gauge
• Yarn needle

GAUGE

14 sts and 12 rows to 4"/10cm over hdc using size H/8 (5mm) hook.
Take time to check gauge.

NOTE

See page 139 for working color changes.

BLANKET

With MC, ch 122. **Row 1** Hdc in 3rd ch from hook and in each ch across—120 sts. Ch 2, turn.
Stripe pattern
Rows 2-12 Hdc in each st across. Join A, ch 2, turn.
Row 13 Hdc in each st across. Join B, ch 1, turn.

Rows 14 and 15 Sc in each st across. Ch 1, turn. After row 15 is completed, join A, ch 2 turn.
Row 16 Hdc in each st across. Join B, ch 1, turn.
Rows 17 and 18 Rep rows 14 and 15. After row 18 is completed, join A, ch 2 turn.
Row 19 Hdc in each st across. Join MC, ch 2, turn.
Rows 20-31 Hdc in each st across. ch 2, turn. After row 31 is completed, join A, ch 2, turn.
Row 32 Hdc in each st across. Join B, ch 1, turn.
Rows 33 and 34 Rep rows 14 and 15. After row 34 is completed, join A, ch 2 turn.
Row 35 Hdc in each st across. Join MC, ch 2, turn.
Rows 36-47 Hdc in each st across. Ch 2, turn. After row 47 is completed, join A, ch 2, turn. Rep rows 13-47 once more, then rows 13-31 once. After last row 31 is completed, do not ch, fasten off.

FINISHING

Lightly block piece to measurements.

Embroidery
Use yarn doubled in needle throughout and make sure to maintain st and row gauge when weaving. For horizontal stitching lines, cut 6 lengths of C. Weave under and over sts along center of each

MC section. For each vertical stitching lines section, cut 3 lengths each of A and B. **First section** Count 14 sts from RH edge. Beg at bottom edge, weave B under and over rows to top edge. *Sk next st and weave A over and under rows to top edge, sk next st and weave B under and over rows to top edge; rep from * once more, end sk next st and weave A over and under rows to top edge. **Second section** Count 23 sts from last A stripe. Beg with an A stripe, work as for first section, reversing colors. **Third section** Count 24 sts from last A stripe of second section. Beg with a B stripe, work as for first section. **Fourth section** Count 22 sts from last A stripe. Beg with an A stripe, work as for first section, reversing colors.

Edging

From RS, join B with a sl st in any corner. **Rnd 1** Ch 2, making sure that work lies flat, hdc evenly around entire edge, working 3 hdc in each corner. Join rnd with a sl st in ch-2. **Rnd 2** Ch 5, turn. Sk next st, sc in next st, *ch 5, sk next 2 sts, sc in next st; rep from * around, sk only 1 st at each corner. Join rnd with a sl st in 1st ch of ch-5. **Rnd 3** Ch 5, turn. *Sc in next ch-5 lp, ch 5; rep from * around. Join rnd with a sl st in first sc. Fasten off.

FINISHED MEASUREMENTS
• 36" x 36"/91.5 x 91.5cm

MATERIALS
• *2 1¾oz/50g (each approx 130yd/119m) of Jaeger Handknits Matchmaker DK (wool) in #887 fuchsia (A), #883 petal (B), #888 parma (C), #882 haze (D), #870 rosy (E), #881 trellis (F) and #876 clarice (G)*
• *Size H/8 (5mm) crochet hook or size to obtain gauge*

GAUGE
20 sts and 11 rows to 4"/10cm over pat st using size H/8 (5mm) hook.
Take time to check gauge.

NOTE
See page 139 for working color changes.

BLANKET
With A, ch 183. **Row 1** Work 2 hdc in 3rd ch from hook, hdc in next 4 ch, * sk next 2 ch, hdc in next 5 ch, work 3 hdc in next ch, hdc in next 5 ch; rep from *, end sk next 2 ch, hdc in next 4 ch, work 2 hdc in last ch—181 sts. Join B, ch 2, turn. **Row 2**
Work 2 hdc in first st, hdc in next 4 sts, * sk next 2 sts, hdc in next 5 sts, work 3 hdc in next st, hdc in next 5 sts; rep from *, end sk next 2 sts, hdc in next 4 sts, work 2 hdc in last st. Join C, ch 2, turn. Rep row 2 for pat st and work in stripe pat as foll: 1 row each C, D, E, F, G, A and B. Work even until piece measures approx 36"/91.5cm, end with 1 row A.

FINISHING
Lightly block piece to measurements.
Edging
From RS with A, join yarn with a sl st in side edge of first row. Making sure that work lies flat, sc evenly along side edge to last row. Fasten off. Rep along opposite side edge.
Pompoms
Make 1½"/4cm in diameter pompoms as foll: 4 using A and 2 each using B, C, D, E, F and G. Referring to photo, sew pompoms to points as shown. *For your child's safety, please ensure that pompoms are sewn securely to blanket.*

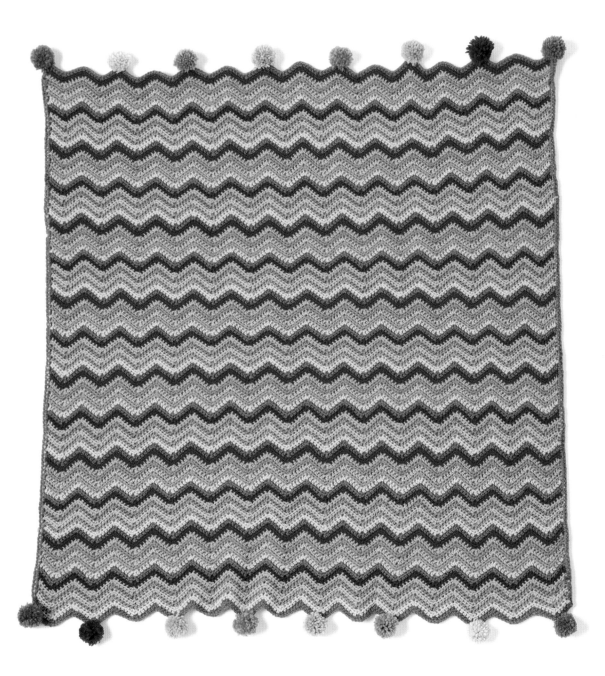

FINISHED MEASUREMENTS
• 30" x 30"/76 x 76cm (not including edging)

MATERIALS
• 6 1¾ oz/50g hanks (each approx 108yd/99m) of Tahki Yarns/Tahki•Stacy Charles, Inc., Cotton Classic (cotton) in #3815 lt. aqua (A) and 3804 teal (B)
• 2 hanks in #3003 off white (C)
• 1 hank in #3786 dark teal (D)
• Size H/8 (5mm) crochet hook or size to obtain gauge
• Yarn needle

GAUGES
• 14 sts and 12 rows to 4"/10cm over hdc using size H/8 (5mm) hook.
• One square to 6"/15cm using size H/8 (5mm) hook.
Take time to check gauges.

SQUARE
(make 25)
With A, ch 24. **Row 1** Hdc in 3rd ch from hook and in each ch across—22 sts. Ch 2, turn. **Row 2** Hdc in each st across. Ch 2, turn. Rep row 2 for pat st and work until a total of 18 rows have been completed. Fasten off. Make 11 more using A, 9 using B and 4 using C.

FINISHING
Lightly block squares to measurements. Referring to photo, sew squares tog.
Embroidery
Refer to photo. Use yarn doubled in needle throughout and make sure to maintain st and row gauge when weaving. Weave under and over every st or row. For horizontal stitching lines, beg at one side edge and end at opposite side edge. Weave C through center row of first, 3rd and 5th rows of squares, then weave D through center row of 2nd and 4th rows of squares; as shown. For vertical stitching lines, beg at bottom edge and end at top edge. Weave C between sts 11 and 12 of squares 1, 3 and 5, then weave D between sts 11 and 12 of squares 2 and 4, as shown.
Edging
From RS, join C with a sl st in center of any side edge. **Rnd 1** Ch 1, making sure that work lies flat, sc evenly around, working 3 sc in each corner. Join rnd with a sl st in first sc. **Rnd 2** Ch 3 (counts as 1 dc), turn. Dc in each st around, working 3 dc in each corner. Join rnd with a sl st in 3rd ch of ch-3. Fasten off.

s q u a r e d a n c e

FINISHED MEASUREMENTS

• 31½" x 32¼"/80 x 82cm (not including border)

MATERIALS

• 4 1¾oz/50g balls (each approx 123yd/113m) of Rowan Yarns Wool Cotton (wool/cotton) in #901 citron (A), #900 antique (B) and #946 elf (C)
• 3 balls in #953 august (D)
• Size H/8 (5mm) crochet hook or size to obtain gauge
• Bobbins
• Yarn needle

GAUGES

• 16 sts and 20 rows to 4"/10cm over sc using size H/8 (5mm) hook.
• One block to 10½" x 10¾"/26.5 x 27.5cm using size H/8 (5mm) hook.
Take time to check gauges.

NOTES

1 See page 139 for working color changes.
2 When working gingham blocks, wind A and C onto two separate bobbins each and B onto one bobbin.

STRIPE BLOCK

(make 4)

With A, ch 43. **Row 1** Sc in 2nd ch from hook and in each ch across—42 sts. Ch 1, turn. **Row 2** Sc in each st across. Join D, ch 1, turn. Rep row 2 for pat st and cont in stripe pat as foll: *work 2 rows each in D, B, C and A; rep from * until a total of 54 rows have been completed. Fasten off.

GINGHAM BLOCK

(make 5)

With A, ch 43. **Row 1** Sc in 2nd ch from hook and in next 13 ch, change to B, sc in next 14 ch, change to A, sc in last 14 ch—42 sts. Ch 1, turn. **Row 2** With A, sc in first 14 sts, with B, sc in next 14 sts, with A, sc in last 14 sts. Ch 1, turn. **Rows 3-18** Rep row 2. When row 18 is completed, change to B, ch 1, turn. **Rows 19-36** With C, sc in first 14 sts, with A, sc in next 14 sts, with C, sc in last 14 sts. Ch 1, turn. When row 36 is completed, change to A, ch 1, turn. **Rows 37-54** Rep row 2. When row 54 is completed, do not ch, fasten off.

FINISHING

Lightly block pieces to measurements.

Embroidery

Use D doubled in needle throughout and make sure to maintain st and row gauge when weaving. For horizontal stitching lines, weave under and over every st between rows 9 and 10, 27 and 28, and 44 and 45. For vertical stitching lines, weave under and over every row between sts 7 and 8, 21 and 22, and 35 and 36. Referring to photo, sew blocks tog.

Border

From RS, join D with a sl st in any corner.

Rnd 1 Ch 1, making sure that work lies flat, sc evenly around, working 3 sc in each corner. Join rnd with a sl st in first sc.

Rnds 2-6 Ch 1, sc in each st around, working 3 sc in each corner st. Join rnd with a sl st in first sc. Fasten off.

FINISHED MEASUREMENTS

• 39" x 37½"/99 x 95cm (not including border)

MATERIALS

• 5 6oz/172g skeins (each approx 326yd/298m) of Red Heart®/Coats&Clark™ TLC Essentials (acrylic) in #2316 winter white (MC) ▣ 4 ▣
• 2 skeins in #2531 light plum (A)
• 1 skein each in #2533 dark plum (B) and #2672 light thyme (C)
• Size H/8 (5mm) crochet hook or size to obtain gauge
• Bobbins
• Yarn needle

GAUGES

• 18 sts to 5"/12.5cm and 10 rows to 4"/10cm over pat st using size H/8 (5mm) hook.
• One block to 13" x 12½"/33 x 31.5cm using size H/8 (5mm) hook.
Take time to check gauges.

NOTES

1 See page 139 for working color changes
2 Wind MC onto one bobbin, and A and B onto two separate bobbins each.

SOLID BLOCK

(make 4)

With MC, ch 48. **Row 1** Sc in 2nd ch from hook, *sk next ch, work 3 sc in next ch, sk next ch; rep from *, end sc in last ch—47 sts. Ch 1, turn. **Row 2** Sc in first st, *sk next st, work 3 sc in next st, sk next st; rep from *, end sc in last st. Ch 1, turn. Rep row 2 for pat st and work until a total of 32 rows have been completed. When row 32 is completed, do not ch, fasten off.

GINGHAM BLOCK

(make 4)

With A, ch 48. **Row 1** Sc in 2nd ch from hook [sk next ch, work 3 sc in next ch, sk next ch] 5 times changing to MC, [sk next ch, work 3 sc in next ch, sk next ch] 5 times changing to A, [sk next ch, work 3 sc in next ch, sk next ch] 5 times, end sc in

last ch—47 sts. Ch 1, turn. **Rows 2-10** Sc in first st, [sk next st, work 3 sc in next st, sk next st] 5 times changing to MC, [sk next st, work 3 sc in next st, sk next st] 5 times changing to A, [sk next st, work 3 sc in next st, sk next st] 5 times, end sc in last st. Ch 1, turn. When row 10 is completed, join B, ch 1, turn. **Rows 11-21** Sc in first st, [sk next st, work 3 sc in next st, sk next st] 5 times changing to A, [sk next st, work 3 sc in next st, sk next st] 5 times changing to B, [sk next st, work 3 sc in next st, sk next st] 5 times, end sc in last st. Ch 1, turn. When row 21 is completed, join A, ch 1, turn. **Rows 22-31** Rep row 2. When row 31 is completed, work with A only, ch 1, turn. **Row 32** Sc in first st, *sk next st, work 3 sc in next st, sk next st; rep from *, end sc in last st. Fasten off.

Lightly block squares to measurements. Referring to photo, sew blocks tog as shown.

Embroidery

Use a single strand of C in needle throughout and make sure to maintain st and row gauge when weaving. For horizontal stitching lines, work from one side edge to the opposite side edge. Weave under and over every st along centers of each gingham block, as shown. For vertical stitching lines, work from bottom edge to top edge. Weave under and over every row along centers of each gingham block, as shown.

Border

From RS, join MC with a sl st in any corner. **Rnd 1** Ch 1, sc in same st as joining, *work 102 sc evenly spaced across edge to corner, work 3 sc in corner; rep from * around, end last rep with 2 sc in beg corner. Join rnd with a sl st in first sc. **Rnd 2** Sl st in sc, ** *sc in next st, ch 4, sk next 2 sts; rep from * to 1 st before corner, sc in next st, ch 3, sk 3 corner sts, sc in next sc; rep from ** around—34 ch-4 sps each side. Join rnd with a sl st in first sc. **Rnd 3** Sl st to center of ch 4, ** *sc in next ch 4-sp, ch 4; rep from * to corner ch-3 sp, work (sc, ch 3, sc) in corner sp; rep from ** around—35 ch-4 sps each side. Join rnd with a sl st. **Rnd 4** Sl st to center of first ch-4 sp, ch 1, sc in same sp, ** *work (3 dc, ch 2, 3 dc) in next ch-4 sp, sc in next ch-4 sp; rep from * to corner ch-3 sp, work (4 dc, ch 3, 4 dc) in corner sp; rep from ** around—17 points each side. Join rnd with a sl st in ch-1. Fasten off, turn. **Rnd 5** From WS, join C with a sl st in center ch of any corner ch-3 sp. Working through front lps only and making sure that work lies flat, sl st in each st and ch around. Join rnd with a sl st in first sl st. Fasten off.

FINISHED MEASUREMENTS

• 23" x 36"/58.5 x 91.5cm (not including border)

MATERIALS

• 4 1¾oz/50g balls (each approx 123yd/113m) of Rowan Yarns Wool Cotton (wool/cotton) in #901 citron (A), #900 antique (B) and #946 elf (C) **4**
• 3 balls in #953 august (D)
• Size G/7 (4.5mm) crochet hook or size to obtain gauge
• Bobbins
• Yarn needle

GAUGE

17 sts and 20 rows to 4"/10cm over sc and gingham pat using size G/6 (4.5mm) hook. *Take time to check gauge.*

NOTES

1 Blanket is made in one piece.
2 See page 139 for working color changes.
3 When working gingham pat, wind A and C onto four separate bobbins each, and B onto three separate bobbins.

BLANKET

With A, ch 99. **Foundation row** Sc in 2nd ch from hook and in each ch across—98 sts. Ch 1, turn

Gingham Pattern
Rows 1-20 *With A, sc in next 14 sts, with B, sc in next 14 sts; rep from *, end with A, sc in last 14 sts. Ch 1, turn. After row 20 has been completed, join C, ch 1, turn.
Rows 21-40 *With C, sc in next 14 sts, with A, sc in next 14 sts; rep from *, end with C, sc in last 14 sts. Ch 1, turn. After row 40 has been completed, join A, ch 1, turn.
Rows 41-60 Rep rows 1-20.
Rows 61-80 Rep rows 21-40.
Rows 81-100 Rep rows 1-20.
Rows 101-120 Rep rows 21-40.
Rows 121-140 Rep rows 1-20.
Rows 141-160 Rep rows 21-40.
Rows 161-180 Rep rows 1-20. After row 180 is competed, do not ch, fasten off.

Lightly block piece to measurements.

Embroidery

Use D doubled in needle throughout and make sure to maintain st and row gauge when weaving. For horizontal stitching lines, weave under and over every st between rows 10 and 11, and 30 and 31 to top. For vertical stitching lines, weave under and over every 2 rows between sts 7 and 8, 21 and 22 across, then cont across as shown.

Border

From RS, join D with a sl st in any corner.

Rnd 1 Ch 2, making sure that work lies flat, hdc evenly around, working 3 hdc in each corner. Join rnd with a sl st in first hdc.

Rnds 2-3 Ch 2, hdc in each st around, working 3 hdc in each corner st. Join rnd with a sl st in first hdc. Fasten off.

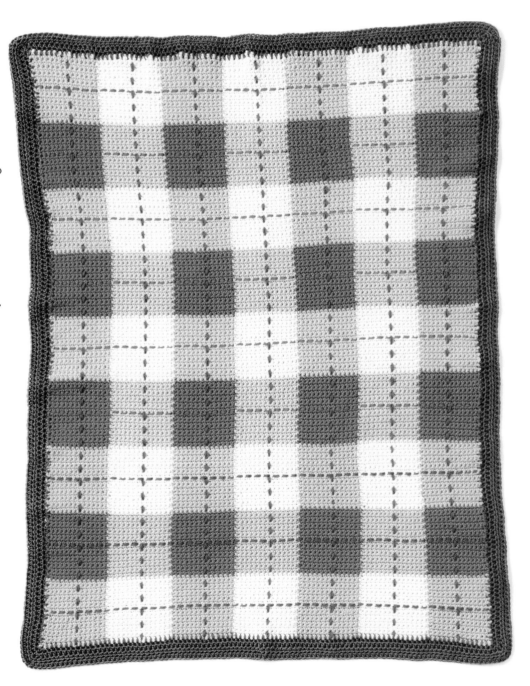

p r e t t y   i n   p i n k

FINISHED MEASUREMENTS
- 35" x 36"/89 x 91.5 (not including border)

MATERIALS
- 9 2½ oz/70g balls (each approx 168yd/154m) of Lion Brand Yarn Co. Microspun (acrylic) in #101 peppermint pink (**3**)
- Size G/6 (4.5mm) crochet hook or size to obtain gauge

GAUGE
27 sts and 15 rows to 7"/17.5cm over cable pat using size G/6 (4.5mm) hook. *Take time to check gauge.*

STITCH GLOSSARY

FPDC (Front Post Double Crochet)
Yo, working from front to back to front, insert hook around post of st of row below, yo and draw up a lp, [yo and draw through 2 lps on hook] twice.

FPTR (Front Post Treble Crochet)
Yo twice, working from front to back to front, insert hook around post of st of row below, yo and draw up a lp, [yo and draw through 2 lps on hook] 3 times.

BPTR (Back Post Treble Crochet)
Yo twice, working from back to front to back, insert hook around post of st of row below, yo and draw up a lp, [yo and draw through 2 lps on hook] 3 times.

CT (Cable Twist)
Sk 2 sts, FPTR around next 2 sts, then FPTR around first skipped st, then 2nd skipped st.

BLANKET

Ch 140. **Foundation row (WS)** Dc in 4th ch from hook and in each ch across—137 sts. Ch 3, turn.

Cable pattern

Row 1 (RS) Dc in first st, [FPDC around next st, dc in next st] twice, FPDC around next st, *[dc in next 2 sts, CT around next 4 sts, dc in next 2 sts, FPDC around next st] twice, [dc in next 2 sts, FPDC around next st] 3 times; rep from * across 4 times, end [dc in next 2 sts, CT around next 4 sts, dc in next 2 sts, FPDC around next st] twice, [dc in next st, FPDC around next st] twice, dc in last st. Ch 3, turn.

Row 2 Dc in first st, [BPTR around next st, dc in next st] twice, BPTR around next st, *[dc in next 2 sts, BPTR around next 4 sts, dc in next 2 sts, BPTR around next st] twice, [dc in next 2 sts, BPTR around next st] 3 times; rep from * across 4 times, end [dc in next 2 sts, BPTR around next 4 sts, dc in next 2 sts, BPTR around next st] twice, [dc in next st, BPTR around next st] twice, dc in last st. Ch 3, turn. Rep rows 1 and 2 for cable pat and work until piece measures 36"/91.5cm from beg, end with row 2. Fasten off.

FINISHING
Lightly block piece to measurements.
Border
From RS, join yarn with a sl st in center of any side edge. **Rnd 1** Ch 1, making sure that work lies flat, sc evenly around entire edge, working 3 sc in each corner. Join rnd with a sl st in first sc. **Rnd 2** Ch 3, dc in each st around, working (2 dc, ch 1, 2 dc) in each corner st. Join rnd with a sl st in 3rd ch of ch-3. **Rnd 3** Ch 1, sc in same st as joining, sc in each st around, working (sc, ch 1, sc) in each corner ch-1 sp. Join rnd with a sl st in first sc. **Rnd 4** Rep rnd 2. **Rnd 5** Ch 1, turn, sc in each st around, working (sc, ch 1, sc) in each corner ch-1 sp. Join rnd with a sl st in first sc. Fasten off.

t r u e   b l u e

FINISHED MEASUREMENTS
• 33" x 36½"/84 x 92.5cm (not including border)

MATERIALS
• 5 5oz/143g skeins (each approx 302yd/277m) of Red Heart®/Coats&Clark™ Kids (acrylic) in #2652 periwinkle (MC)
• 1 3oz/85g skein (each approx 200yd/183m) of Red Heart®/Coats&Clark™ Baby Terri (acrylic/nylon) in #9101 white (CC)
• Size H/8 (5mm) crochet hook or size to obtain gauge

GAUGE
16 sts to 5"/12.5cm and 14 rows to 4"/10cm over diamond bobble pat using size H/8 (5mm) hook.
Take time to check gauge.

NOTES
1 Blanket is made vertically.
2 Push all tr sts to RS as you work.

BLANKET
With CC, ch 119. **Foundation row 1 (WS)** Hdc in 3rd ch from hook and each ch across—117 sts. Ch 1, turn. **Foundation row 2** Working though back lps only, sc in each st across. Fasten off, do not turn.

Diamond bobble pattern
Row 1 (RS) From RS, join MC with a sl st in first st at RH edge. Ch 3, dc in each st across. Ch 1, turn.
Row 2 Working through front lps only, sc in each st across—117 sts. Ch 1, turn.
Row 3 Sc in first 2 sts, *sc in next 4 sts, tr in next st, sc in next 3 sts; rep from *, end sc in last 3 sts. Ch 1, turn.
Row 4 Sc in first 3 sts, *sc in next 2 sts, tr in next st, sc in next, tr in next st, sc in next 3 sts; rep from *, end sc in last 2 sts. Ch 1, turn.
Row 5 Sc in first 2 sts, *sc in next 2 sts, tr in next st, sc in next 3 sts, tr in next st, sc in next st; rep from * across, end sc in last 3 sts. Ch 1, turn.
Row 6 Sc in first 3 sts, *tr in next st, sc in next 5 sts, tr in next st, sc in next st; rep from * across, end sc in last 2 sts. Ch 1, turn.
Row 7 Sc in first 2 sts, *tr in next st, sc in next 3 sts, tr in next st, sc in 3 sts; rep from * across, end tr in next st, sc in last 2 sts. Ch 1, turn.
Row 8 Rep row 6.
Row 9 Rep row 5.
Row 10 Rep row 4.
Row 11 Rep row 3.
Row 12 Working through front lps only, dc in each st across. Fasten off, do not turn.
Row 13 From RS, join CC with a sl st in first st at RH edge. Ch 2, hdc in each st across. Ch 1, turn.

Row 14 Working through back lps only, sc in each st across. Fasten off, do not turn. Rep rows 1-14 six more times, end with row 14. Fasten off.

FINISHING
Lightly block piece to measurements.
Border
From RS, join MC with a sl st in center of any side edge. **Rnd 1** Ch 1, making sure that work lies flat, sc evenly around entire edge, working 3 sc in each corner. Join rnd with a sl st in first sc. **Rnd 2** Ch 3, working through back lps only, dc in each st around, working (2 dc, ch 1, 2 dc) in center st of each corner. Join rnd with a sl st in 3rd ch of ch-3. **Rnd 3** Ch 1, working through back lps only, sc in same sp as joining, sc in each st around, working 3 sc in each corner ch-1 sp. Join rnd with a sl st in first sc. **Rnd 4** Ch 1, working through back lps only, sc in same sp as joining, sc in each st around, working 3 sc in center st of each corner. Join rnd with a sl st in first sc. **Rnd 5** Working through front lps only and making sure that work lies flat, sl st each st around, working 3 sl sts in center st of each corner. Join rnd with a sl st in first sl st. Fasten off.

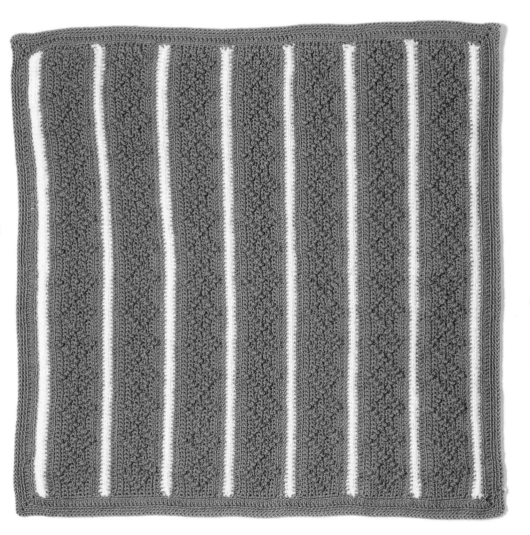

FINISHED MEASUREMENTS

• 34" x 35"/86.5 x 89cm (not including border)

MATERIALS

• 5 3oz/85g skeins (each approx 170yd/156m) of Red Heart®/Coats&Clark™ Super Saver (acrylic) in #311 white (MC) (4)
• 1 4oz/115g skein (each approx 222yd/203m) of Red Heart® Hokey Pokey (acrylic) each in #7107 bubblegum (A), #7108 tangerine (B), #7109 sunshine (C), #7110 spearmint (D), #7111 blue bonnet (F) and #7113 periwinkle (E) (4)
• Size H/8 (5mm) crochet hook or size to obtain gauge

GAUGE

12 sts and 15 rows to 4"/10cm over pat st using size H/8 (5mm) hook.
Take time to check gauge.

NOTE

See page 139 for working color changes.

STITCH GLOSSARY

LSC (Long Single Crochet)
Insert hook in designated st 3 rows below, yo, draw up a lp, yo and draw through 2 lps on hook to complete sc; sk sc below LSC.

LVS (Long V-Stitch)
(worked over 3 sts)
LSC in st to left of st, sc in next st, LSC in same base as first LSC—long v-stitch formed.

BLANKET

With MC, ch 102. **Foundation row 1 (RS)** Sc in 2nd ch from hook and each ch across—101 sts. Ch 1, turn. **Foundation row 2** Sc in each st across. Join A, ch 1, turn.

Pattern stitch

Row 1 (RS) With A, sc in first 3 sts, * LSC over next st, [sc in next st, LSC over next st] 3 times, sc in next 5 sts, [LVS over next 3 sts, sc in next 5 sts] 4 times; rep from * twice, end LSC over next st, [sc in next st, LSC over next st] 3 times, sc in last 3 sts. Ch 1, turn.

Row 2 With A, sc in each st across. Join MC, ch 1, turn.

Row 3 Work in back loops only. With MC, sc in first 3 sts, *[sc in next st, LSC over next st] 3 times, sc in next 6 sts, [LVS over 3 sts, sc in next 5 sc] 4 times; rep from * twice, end [sc in next st, LSC over next st] 3 times, sc in last 4 sts. Ch 1, turn.

Row 4 With MC, sc in each st across. Join B, ch 1, turn. Rep rows 1-4 for pat st and work in stripe pat as foll: work rows 1 and 2 using B, C, D, E, F, A, B, C, D, E, F, and work rows 3 and 4 with MC only, end with row 4. Using MC only and working through both lps on each row, rep rows 1-4 until piece measures 24"/61cm from beg, end with row 4. Cont in pat st and work in stripe pat as foll: work rows 1 and 2 using [F, E, D, C, B, A] twice, and work rows 3 and 4 with MC only, end with row 4. Fasten off.

FINISHING

Lightly block piece to measurements.

Border

From RS, join MC with a sl st in center of any side edge. **Rnd 1** Ch 1, sc in same st as joining, *ch 1, sk next st (or row), sc in next st (or row); rep from * around, working (sc, ch 2, sc) in each corner. Join rnd with a sl st in first sc. Ch 1, turn. **Rnds 2-5** *Sc in next ch-1 sp, ch 1; rep from * around, working (sc, ch 2, sc) in each corner ch-2 sp. Join rnd with a sl st in first sc. Ch 1, turn. After rnd 5 is completed, join rnd with a sl st in first sc, fasten off.

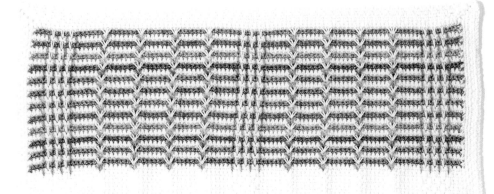

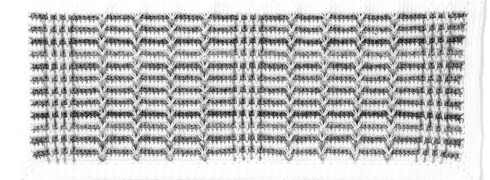

crème de la crème

FINISHED MEASUREMENTS

• 34" x 38"/86.5 x 96.5cm

MATERIALS

• 3 3oz/86g skeins (each approx 175yd/160m) of Caron International Simply Soft (acrylic) in #2602 off white
• Size H/8 (5mm) crochet hook or size to obtain gauge
• ½yd/.5m of 58"/147.5cm-wide blue and white toile fabric
• Off white sewing thread
• Sewing needle
• Straight pins

GAUGE

12 sts and 10 rows to 4"/10cm over hdc using size H/8 (5mm) hook.
Take time to check gauge.

NOTE

Blanket is made vertically.

BLANKET

Ch 116. **Row 1** Hdc in 3rd ch from hook and in each ch across—114sts. Ch 2, turn. **Row 2** Hdc in each st across. Ch 2, turn. Rep row 2 for pat st and work until piece measures 34"/86.5cm from beg. Fasten off.

FINISHING

Lightly block piece to measurements.
Fabric binding
Cut two strips of toile 4" x 35"/10 x 89cm (top and bottom) and two strips 4" x 39"/10 x 99cm (sides). For each strip, fold in half lengthwise and press. Turn each long edge ½"/1.3cm to WS; press. Fold each short end ½"/1.3cm to WS; press. Beg at bottom edge. Unfold strip and place on work surface. Place bottom edge of blanket along fold line, side edges even. Fold bottom edge of strip to RS of blanket. Pin, taking care not to stretch blanket sts. Turn blanket to first side edge and pin strip in the same manner, then at RH edge, fold end of strip into a mitered corner; pin. Turn blanket to top edge, pin strip, then miter corner at RH edge. Turn blanket to second side edge, pin strip, then miter corner at RH edge. Unpin bottom strip at RH edge, then fold into a mitered corner on top of side strip. Working through all thicknesses, sew binding along top folded edges. Sew mitered corners in place.

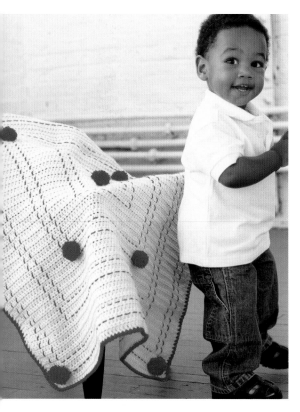

FINISHED MEASURMENTS

- 34½" x 38"/87.5 x 96.5cm (not including edging)

MATERIALS

- 2 3½/100g skeins (each approx 210yd/192m) of Patons® Decor (acrylic/wool) in #1602 aran (MC)
- 1 skein in #1714 barn red (CC)
- Size H/8 (5mm) crochet hook or size to obtain gauge
- Yarn needle

GAUGE

12 sts and 10 rows to 4"/10cm over hdc using size H/8 (5mm) hook.
Take time to check gauge.

BLANKET

With MC, ch 106. **Row 1** Hdc in 3rd ch from hook and in each ch across—104 sts. Ch 2, turn. **Row 2** Hdc in each st across. Ch 2, turn. Rep row 2 for pat st and work even until piece measures 38"/96.5cm from beg. Fasten off.

FINISHING

Lightly block piece to measurements.
Embroidery
Use a single strand of CC in needle throughout. Weave under and over every st or row, making make sure to maintain st and row gauge. Referring to photo, note how all stitching lines are woven over and under the same sts vertically and horizontally. **Rnd 1** Count 4 sts from side edge and beg weaving 3 rows from bottom edge. Weave to within 3 rows of top edge, then turn corner. Cont to weave in the same manner to beg. **Rnd 2** Weave stitching lines 3 sts and 3 rows from rnd 1. **Rnd 3** Weave stitching lines 9 sts and 7 rows from rnd 2. **Rnd 4** Weave stitching lines 3 sts and 3 rows from rnd 3. **Rnd 5** Weave stitching lines 9 sts and 7 rows from rnd 4. **Rnd 6** Weave stitching lines 3 sts and 3 rows from rnd 5. **Rnd 7** Weave stitching lines 9 sts and 7 rows from rnd 6. **Rnd 8** Weave stitching lines 3 sts and 3 rows from rnd 7.

Edging
From RS, join CC with a sl st in center of any side edge. **Rnd 1** Ch 1, making sure that work lies flat, sc evenly around entire edge, working 3 sc in each corner. Join rnd with a sl st in first sc. Fasten off.

Pompoms
Using CC, make nine pompoms 1½"/4cm in diameter. Referring to photo, sew pompoms in place, as shown. *For your child's safety, please ensure that pompoms are sewn securely to blanket.*

b a b y   l o v e

• 32" x 36"/81 x 91.5cm

MATERIALS
• 6 3½oz/100g balls (each approx 207yd/188m) of Lion Brand Yarn Co. Cotton-Ease (cotton/acrylic) in #106 ice blue (MC) **3**
• 1 ball in #100 vanilla (CC)
• Size H/8 (5mm) crochet hook or size to obtain gauge
• Yarn needle
• One package of white satin blanket binding
• One package of white jumbo rick rack
• White sewing thread
• Sewing needle
• Straight pins

GAUGE
12 sts and 16 rows to 4"/10cm over sc using size H/8 (5mm) hook.
Take time to check gauge.

BLANKET
With MC, ch 97. **Row 1** Sc in 2nd ch from hook and in each ch across—-96 sts. Ch 1, turn. **Row 2** Sc in each st across. Ch 1, turn. Rep row 2 for pat st and work even until piece measures 36"/91.5cm from beg. Fasten off.

FINISHING
Lightly block piece to measurements.
Embroidery
Use CC doubled in needle throughout and make sure to maintain st and row gauge when weaving. Refer to photo. Beg 2"/5cm from RH bottom corner. Working diagonally, weave under and over sts and rows to opposite side edge. Space rem diagonal stitching lines approx 8"/20.5cm apart.
Binding
Beg at bottom edge. Unfold binding and place on work surface. Place bottom edge of blanket along fold line so binding extends ½"/1.3cm from RH edge of blanket. Fold bottom edge of binding to RS of blanket. Pin, taking care not to stretch blanket sts. Turn blanket to first side edge and pin binding, mitering binding at corner; pin. Cont around next two sides. Cut binding so 1"/2.5cm extends from LH edge of blanket, then fold into a mitered corner. Working through all thicknesses, sew binding along top edges. Sew last mitered corner to secure it in place. Sew rick rack around binding as shown.

petal pretty

FINISHED MEASURMENTS
• 34½" x 38"/87.5 x 96.5cm (without edging)

MATERIALS
• 5 1¾oz/50g balls (each approx 114yd/105m) of Wendy/Berroco, Inc.
• Velvet Touch (nylon) in #1201 cream (MC) ⬤4
• 1 ball each in #1209 pink (A) and #1205 bright pink (B)
• Size H/8 (5mm) crochet hook or size to obtain gauge

GAUGE
12 sts and 10 rows to 4"/10cm over hdc using size H/8 (5mm) hook.
Take time to check gauge.

BLANKET
With MC, ch 106. **Row 1** Hdc in 2nd ch from hook and in each ch across—104 sts. Ch 2, turn. **Row 2** Hdc in each st across. Ch 2, turn. Rep row 2 for pat st and work until piece measures 38"/96.5cm from beg. Fasten off.

LARGE FLOWERS
(make 2)
With A, ch 5. Join ch with a sl st forming a ring. **Rnd 1** Ch 1, work 14 sc over ring. Join rnd with a sl st in ch-1. **Rnd 2** [Ch 4, sk next 2 sts, sl st in next st] 4 times, end ch 4, sk last 2 sts, sl st in first ch of ch-4— 5 ch-4 lps. **Rnd 3** Ch 1 (counts as 1 sc), work (dc, 2 tr, dc, sc) in first ch-4 sp, * work (sc, dc, 2 tr, dc, sc) in next ch-4 sp; rep from * around 4 times. Join rnd with a sl st in ch-1. **Rnd 4** [Ch 5, sl st between next 2 sc (between petals)] 4 times, end ch 5, sl st in first ch of beg ch-5—5 ch-5 lps. Fasten off. **Rnd 5** Join B with a sl st in any ch-5 lp with a sl st, ch 1, *work (sc, 2 dc, 2 tr, 2 dc, sc) in next ch-5 lp; rep from * around 5 times. Join rnd with a sl st in ch-1. Fasten off.

SMALL FLOWERS
(make 4)
With A, ch 5. Join ch with a sl st forming a ring. Rep rnds 1-3 as for large flower. Fasten off. Make 2 more using A and make 1 using B.

BOBBLE

(make 6)

With A, ch 2 leaving a long tail for sewing.
Row 1 In 2nd ch from hook work (yo, draw up a lp, yo, draw through 2 lps on hook) 4 times, yo and draw through all 5 lps on hook. Fasten off leaving a long tail for sewing. Make 5 more using B. *For your child's safety, please ensure that bobbles are sewn securely to blanket.*

FINISHING

Lightly block piece to measurements.
Edging
From RS, join B with a sl st in center of any side edge. **Rnd 1** Ch 2, making sure that work lies flat, hdc around entire edge working 3 hdc in each corner. Join rnd with a sl st in first hdc. **Rnd 2** Ch 3, dc in each st around, working 3 dc in each corner. Join rnd with a sl st in first dc. **Rnd 3** Ch 1, sc in same st as joining, *sk next st, work 5 dc in next st, sk next st, sc in next st; rep from * around, working 5 dc in each corner. Join rnd with a sl st in ch-1. Fasten off. Referring to photo, sew on flowers with bobble centers as shown.

f i n e   l i n e s

FINISHED MEASUREMENTS

• 28" x 34"/71 x 86cm

MATERIALS

• *5 1¾oz/50g balls (each approx 99yd/90m) of Rowan Yarns All Seasons Cotton (cotton/acrylic/microfibre) in #199 ravish (MC)* **4**
• *2 balls each in #197 limedrop (A), #178 organic (B) and #185 jazz (C)*
• *Size I/9 (5.5mm) crochet hook or size to obtain gauge*

GAUGE

12 sts and 10 rows to 4"/10cm over hdc using size I/9 (5.5mm) hook.
Take time to check gauge.

NOTE

See page 139 for working color changes.

BLANKET

With MC, ch 86. **Row 1** Hdc in 3rd ch from hook and in each ch across—84 sts. Ch 2, turn. **Row 2** Hdc in each st across. Ch 2, turn. Rep row 2 for pat st. Work for 1 more row.

Stripe Pattern

Bottom section Work 1 row A, 2 rows MC, 2 rows A, 2 rows MC, 4 rows A, 2 rows MC, 2 rows A, [1 row MC, 1 row A] twice, 2 rows MC, 2 rows A and 5 rows MC. Change to B.

Center section Work 1 row B, 2 rows MC, 2 rows B, 2 rows MC, 4 rows B, 2 rows MC, 2 rows B, [1 row MC, 1 row B] twice, 2 rows MC, 2 rows B and 5 rows MC. Change to C.

Top section Work 1 row C, 2 rows MC, 2 rows C, 2 rows MC, 4 rows C, 2 rows MC, 2 rows C, [1 row MC, 1 row C] twice, 2 rows MC, 2 rows C and 3 rows MC. Fasten off.

FINISHING

Lightly block piece to measurements.

Edging

From RS, join B with a sl st in any corner, ch 1. **Rnd 1** Making sure that work lies flat, sc evenly around entire edge, working 3 sc in each corner. Join rnd with a sl st in ch-1. Fasten off.

FINISHED MEASUREMENTS
• 34" x 36"/86 x 91.5cm

MATERIALS
• 2 1¾oz/50g hanks (each approx 108yd/99m) of Tahki Yarns/Tahki•Stacy Charles, Inc., Cotton Classic (cotton) in #3873 royal blue (A), #3805 aqua (C), #3450 fuchsia (F), #3841 light blue (I) and #3715 chartreuse (J) **4**
• 1 hank each in #3003 off white (B), #3002 black (D), #3351 coral (E), #3936 lavender (G) and #3995 wine (H)
• Size H/8 (5mm) crochet hook or size to obtain gauge

GAUGE
15 sts and 13 rows to 4"/10cm over hdc using size H/8 (5mm) hook.
Take time to check gauge.

NOTES
See page 139 for working color changes.

BLANKET
With A, ch 130. **Row 1** Hdc in 3rd ch from hook and in each ch across—128 sts. Join B, ch 2, turn. **Row 2** Hdc in each st across. Join C, ch 2, turn. Rep row 2 for pat st and work in stripe pat.
Stripe Pattern
* Work 1 row C, 1 row B, 8 rows C, 1 row D, 1 row E, 8 rows F,2 rows D, 2 rows G, 3 rows E, 6 rows H, 1 row B, 3 rows I, 1 row D, 2 rows A, 1 row E, 2 rows A, 1 row B, 1 row I, 8 rows J, 1 row A and 1 row I *, end 1 row A and 1 row B. Rep between * once more. Fasten off.

FINISHING
Lightly block piece to measurements.
Edging
From RS, join B with a sl st in any corner, ch 1. Rnd 1 Making sure that work lies flat, sc evenly around entire edge, working 3 sc in each corner. Join rnd with a sl st in ch-1. Fasten off.

THE SLIP KNOT

1 Begin to crochet by making a slip knot. Make a loop several inches [or centimeters] from the end of the yarn. Insert the hook through the loop and catch the tail with the end.

2 Pull the yarn through the loop on the hook.

CROCHET HOOKS

US	METRIC
14 steel	.60mm
12 steel	.75mm
10 steel	1.00mm
6 steel	1.50mm
5 steel	1.75mm
B/1	2.25mm
C/2	2.75mm
D/3	3.25mm
E/4	3.50mm
F/5	3.75mm
G/6	4.00mm
H/8	5.00mm
I/9	5.50mm
J/10	6.00mm
K/10.5	6.50mm
L/11	8.00mm

YARN SELECTION

For an exact reproduction of the projects photographed, use the yarn listed in the "Materials" section of the pattern. We've chosen yarns that are readily available in the U.S. and Canada at the time of printing. The Resources list on page 144 provides addresses of yarn distributors. Contact them for the name of a retailer in your area.

YARN SUBSTITUTION

You may wish to substitute yarns. Perhaps you view small-scale projects as a chance to incorporate leftovers from your yarn stash, or the yarn specified may not be available in your area. You'll need to crochet to the given gauge to obtain the crocheted measurements with a substitute yarn (see "Gauge" on this page). Be sure to consider how the fiber content of the substitute yarn will affect the comfort and the ease of care of your projects.

To facilitate yarn substitution, yarns are graded by the standard stitch gauge obtained in single crochet. You'll find a grading number in the "Materials" section of the pattern, immediately following the fiber type of the yarn. Look for a substitute yarn that falls into the same category. The suggested hook size and gauge on the yarn label should be comparable to that on the "Standard Yarn Weight System" chart (see page 139).

After you've successfully gauge-swatched a substitute yarn, you'll need to figure out how much of the substitute yarn the project requires. First, find the total length of the original yarn in the pattern (multiply number of balls by yards/meters per ball). Divide this figure by the new yards/meters per ball (listed on the yarn label). Round up to the next whole number. The answer is the number of balls required.

GAUGE

It is always important to crochet a gauge swatch, and it is even more so with garments to ensure proper fit.

Patterns usually state gauge over a 4"/10cm span, however it's beneficial to make a larger test swatch. This gives a more precise stitch gauge, a better idea of the appearance and drape of the crocheted fabric, and gives you a chance to familiarize yourself with the stitch pattern.

The type of hook used—wood, plastic or metal—will influence gauge, so crochet your swatch with the hook you plan to use for the project. Try different hook sizes until your sample measures the required number of stitches and rows. To get fewer stitches to the inch/cm, use a larger hook; to get more stitches to the inch/cm, use a smaller hook.

It's a good idea to keep your gauge swatch in order to test blocking and cleaning methods.

FOLLOWING CHARTS

Charts are a convenient way to follow colorwork patterns at a glance. When crocheting back and forth in rows, read charts from right to left on right side (RS) rows and from left to right on wrong side (WS) rows, repeating any stitch and row repeats as directed in the pattern. Posting a self-adhesive note under your working row is an easy way to keep track of your place.

FINISHING

Since blankets are frequently worked in one piece, keep finishing in mind when beginning your blanket project.

1 Because the back-side of the fabric will be seen when the blanket is used, you must be ready for the reverse to be on display. Think about using a stitch that is reversible, or one that looks good on both sides.

2 Consider adding border stitches to your blanket so that it has a built-in finish (many border stitches will also help the blanket lie flat).

3 When adding a new yarn, be careful to do so at a place where you can easily weave the ends in, such as the sides, as there is frequently no "wrong side" on a blanket.

4 Consider adding a fabric backing as a whimsical and practical accent to your fine handwork.

COLORWORK CROCHETING

Three main types of colorwork are explored in this book: stripes, intarsia and stranding.

Stripes

When working in single crochet, change color by drawing the new color through 2 loops on hook to complete the last single crochet, then working the next stitch with the new color, or, if at the end of the row, chain and turn.

For half double crochet, draw new color through 3 loops on hook to complete last half double crochet, work the next stitch with the new color, or, if at the end of the row, chain and turn.

When working in double crochet, draw new color through last 2 loops on hook to complete last double crochet, work the next stitch with the new color, or, if at the end of the row, chain and turn.

To prevent lumpy seams, do not make knots when changing colors. Instead, leave a long tail of yarn, then weave in tails after piece is completed and before sewing blocks together.

Intarsia

All the Argyle designs are worked with separate bobbins of individual colors so

CHAIN

1 Pass yarn over the hook and catch it with the hook.

2 Draw yarn through the loop on the hook.

3 Repeat steps 1 and 2 to make a chain.

STANDARD YARN WEIGHT SYSTEM						
Categories of yarn, gauge ranges and recommended needle and hook sizes						
Yarn Weight Symbol & Category Names	**1** Super Fine	**2** Fine	**3** Light	**4** Medium	**5** Bulky	**6** Super Bulky
Type of Yarns in Category	Sock, Fingering, Baby	Sport, Baby	DK, Light Worsted	Worsted, Afghan, Aran	Chunky, Craft, Rug	Super Bulky, Roving
Knit Gauge Range* in Stockinette Stitch to 4 inches	27–32 sts	23–26 sts	21–24 sts	16–20 sts	12–15 sts	6–11 sts
Recommended Needle in Metric Size Range	2.25–3.25 mm	3.25–3.75 mm	3.75–4.5 mm	4.5–5.5 mm	5.5–8 mm	9–15 mm and larger
Recommended Needle U.S. size range	1 to 3	3 to 5	5 to 7	7 to 9	9 to 11	11 to 19 and larger
Crochet Gauge* Ranges in Single Crochet to 4 inch	21–32 sts	16–20 sts	12–17 sts	11–14 sts	8–11 sts	5–9 sts
Recommended Hook in Metric Size Range	2.25–3.5 mm	3.5–4.5 mm	4.5–5.5 mm	5.5–6.5 mm	6.5–9 mm	9–12 mm and larger
Recommended Hook U.S. Size Range	B-1 to E-4	E-4 to 7	7 to I-9	I-9 to K-10½	K-10½ to M-13	M-13 to P-16 and larger

* GUIDELINES ONLY: The above reflect the most commonly used gauges and needle or hook sizes for specific yarn categories.

SINGLE CROCHET

1 Insert hook through top two loops of a stitch. Pass yarn over hook and draw up a loop—two loops on hook.

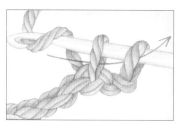

2 Pass yarn over hook and draw through both loops on hook.

3 Continue in the same way, inserting hook into each stitch.

there are no long strands of yarn. When changing color, pick up new color from under dropped color to prevent holes.

BLOCKING

Blocking is a crucial finishing step in the crocheting process. It is the best way to shape pattern pieces and smooth crocheted edges in preparation for sewing together. Most designs retain their shape if the blocking stages in the instructions are followed carefully. Choose a blocking method according to the instructions on the yarn care label, and when in doubt, test-block your gauge swatch.

Wet Block Method

Using rust-proof pins, pin pieces to measurements on a flat surface and lightly dampen using a spray bottle. Allow to dry before removing pins.

Steam Block Method

With wrong sides facing, pin pieces. Steam lightly, holding the iron 2"/5cm above the piece. Do not press or it will flatten stitches.

CARE

Refer to the yarn label for the recommended cleaning method. Many of the projects in the book can be either washed by hand, or in the machine on a gentle or wool cycle, using lukewarm water with a mild detergent. Do not agitate or soak for more than 10 minutes. Rinse gently with tepid water, then fold in a towel and gently press the water out. Lay flat to dry, away from excess heat and light. Check the yarn label for any specific care instructions such as dry cleaning or tumble drying.

MAKING POMPOMS

POMPOM TEMPLATE

2"/5cm

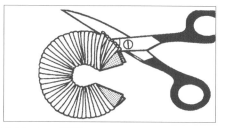

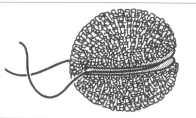

Note: For the safety and protection of your child, it is important to secure all pompoms and bobbles to the baby blanket design. We recommend firmly tugging each pompom and bobble after each one is sewn on to ensure that they're secure.

1 Following the template, cut two circular pieces of cardboard.

2 Hold the two circles together and wrap the yarn tightly around the cardboard several times. Secure and carefully cut the yarn.

3 Tie a piece of yarn tightly between the two circles. Remove the cardboard and trim the pompom to the desired size.

CROCHETING GLOSSARY

decrease 1 dc [Yo. Insert hook into next st and draw up a lp. Yo and draw through 2 lps] twice, yo and draw through all 3 lps on hook.

decrease 1 hdc [Yo, insert hook into next st and draw up a lp] twice, yo and draw through all 5 lps on hook.

decrease 1 sc [Insert hook into next st and draw up a lp] twice, yo and draw through all 3 lps on hook.

increase 1 stitch Work 2 sts in 1 st.

join yarn with a dc Make a slip knot, then yo. Insert hook into st. Yo and draw up a lp. [Yo and draw through 2 lps on hook] twice.

join yarn with a hdc Make a slip knot, then yo. Insert hook into st. Yo and draw up a lp. Yo and draw through 3 lps on hook.

join yarn with a sc Make a slip knot. Insert hook into st. Yo and draw up a lp. Yo and draw through 2 lps on hook.

join yarn with a sl st Make a slip knot. Insert hook into st. Yo and draw up a lp and draw through lp on hook.

HALF-DOUBLE CROCHET

1 Pass yarn over hook. Insert hook through the top two loops of a stitch.

2 Pass yarn over hook and draw up a loop—three loops on hook. Pass yarn over hook.

3 Draw through all three loops on hook.

CROCHET ABBREVIATIONS

approx approximately
beg begin(ning)
CC contrasting color
ch chain(s)
cont continu(e)(ing)
dc double crochet (UK: tr treble)
dec decrease(ing) (see glossary)
g gram(s)
hdc half double crochet (UK: htr half treble)
inc increas(e)(ing) (see glossary)

lp(s) loop(s)
m meter(s)
mm millimeter(s)
MC main color
oz ounce(s)
pat(s) pattern(s)
rem remain(s)(ing)
rep repeat
rnd(s) round(s)
RS right side(s)
sc single crochet (UK: dc double crochet)
sk skip
sl slip
sl st slip st (UK: sc single crochet)
st(s) stitch(es)

tog together
tr treble crochet (UK: dtr double treble)
WS wrong side(s)
yd yard(s)
yo yarn over
***** = repeat directions following * as many times as indicated.
[ ] = repeat directions inside brackets as many times as indicated.
( ) = work directions contained inside parentheses in st indicated.

DOUBLE CROCHET

1 Pass yarn over hook. Insert hook through the top two loops of a stitch.

2 Pass yarn over hook and draw up a loop—three loops on hook.

3 Pass yarn over hook and draw it through the first two loops on the hook, pass yarn over hook and draw through the remaining two loops. Continue in the same way, inserting hook into each stitch.

CHAIN STITCH

acknowledgements

I have always loved babies and find them absolutely irresistible and a constant source of inspiration. So with that in mind, I want to thank my daughter Heather and her husband John for giving me my very own little inspiration, my grandson Johnny. He is always happy to see me and never minds when I wrap him up in my latest creation. He even enjoys our trips to the local yarn shop, where he looks at all the colors and pulls the balls of yarn to the floor. Thank you, Heather and John, for such a living doll.

I also want to thank the many crocheters and superb craftswomen who had the time and patience to make many of the blankets in this book: Dorothy Pippin, Cheryl Roberts, Sharon Roth, Kandi Weider, and especially Anne Mitchell, for her tireless devotion to my project—I couldn't have pulled this off without you. A huge thank-you to my cousin Jim for not only making a perfect blanket but for lending an understanding ear when the crocheting gets tough. Judy Timmer and Jane Lind for their expert crocheting and willingness to work many nights to get things done on time. Last but not least, I send a great big thank-you to Joyce Nordstrom, who became my eyes and hands on this project. Not only did Joyce coordinate the projects, but she helped with pattern and color selection as well— she always knows what I want.

My gift of creativity is only able to fly because of my number one supporter, my husband Tom Noggle.

He never complains about the boxes of yarn and the late nights of work and always manages to make me laugh. Many thanks to my dearest friends—Dieter, Uschi, Christine and Henry—for putting up with my crocheting at the dinner table (because I needed to finish just one more row) and loving me even when I had to keep working instead of coming out to play. And to my mom, Jean, and my sister Rajeana, because they would love me even if I wasn't family.

Finally I want to thank everyone at Sixth&Spring Books who has helped me through this project: Michelle Lo for keeping me on track; Chi Ling Moy for her incredible book design and art direction; Pat Harste and Carla Scott, who are the best technical editors. I also want to extend my gratitude to Dan Howell and Mary Helt for making my designs look so good. Most importantly, I'd like to thank Trisha Malcolm, who continues to be one of my biggest supporters and a true friend. Without her, none of this would be possible.

Photography by Mary Siedman

r e s o u r c e s

Bernat®
distributed by
Spinrite, Inc.

Berroco, Inc.
14 Elmdale Road
PO Box 367
Uxbridge, MA 01569

Classic Elite Yarns
300 Jackson Street
Lowell, MA 01852

Coats&Clark, Inc.
Attn: Consumer Service
PO Box 12229
Greenville, SC 29612-0229

Caron International
1481 West 2nd Street
Washington, NC 27889

Dale of Norway
N16 W23390 Stoneridge Drive
Waukesha, WI 53188

Jaeger Handknits
4 Townsend West, Suite 8
Nashua, NH 03063

Lion Brand Yarn Co.
34 West 15th Street
New York, NY 10011

Patons® **Yarns**
PO Box 40
Listowel, ON N4W3H3
Canada

Red Heart®
distributed by
Coats&Clark, Inc.™

Rowan Yarns
4 Townsend West, Suite 8
Nashua, NH 03063

Spinrite, Inc.
PO Box 40
Listowel, ON N4W3H3
Canada

Tahki Yarns
distributed by
Tahki•Stacy Charles, Inc.

Tahki•Stacy Charles, Inc.
8000 Cooper Ave.
Brooklyn, NY 11222

Wendy
distributed by
Berroco, Inc.